Sat 17.2.05
Cash Sale
to
Pieter Zwart
Arlington
a History
and Guide
1st Ed. 1973
Code x 8
B

D1425980

This book did belong to Jack
but I have been given it
for a loving memory of him
July 25th 1991.

ISLINGTON:
A History and Guide

ISLINGTON:
A History and Guide

PIETER ZWART

SIDGWICK & JACKSON
LONDON

First published in Great Britain in 1973
by Sidgwick and Jackson Limited
Copyright © 1973 by Pieter Zwart

ISBN 0 283 97937 2

Printed in Great Britain by
Eden Fisher (Southend) Ltd
for Sidgwick and Jackson Limited
1 Tavistock Chambers, Bloomsbury Way
London WC1A 2SG

*For C, who first came to Islington
in 1964*

Acknowledgements

MANY have helped with advice and information on the past of Islington which includes Finsbury. I would like to thank the Marquess of Northampton and Miss Olive Lloyd Baker for answering questions about their families; Mr Eric Willats for allowing me to see his manuscript on Islington, Mr John Ferris his study of Barnsbury, Mr Christopher Whittaker his thesis on the Thornhill estate, and Mr David Wager his planning report of 1965 on Barnsbury.

I am grateful to Miss Margaret Drabble and her publishers, Weidenfeld & Nicolson, for permission to quote the passage from *Jerusalem the Golden* (1967), to Mr H. V. Morton and his publishers, Methuen & Co. Ltd for permission to quote the passage from *The Heart of London*, and to John Murray (Publishers) Ltd for permission to quote from John Betjeman's *Collected Poems*.

I am indebted to Mr C. A. Elliott, Chief Librarian of Islington Public Libraries and his staff for their kindness and patience in helping me in my search for information about the history of Islington. In particular I would like to thank Mr E. Willats, Reference Librarian of Islington, for his suggestions and criticism of the history of Islington proper, and Mrs E. V. Lewis, Reference Librarian of Finsbury for her encouraging advice and criticism of the history of Finsbury. Any errors and omissions are mine alone.

I am grateful to Mr Lonsdale, Librarian of *The Times* and his staff for their help with some teasing questions; and to Mr G. Phillips for compiling the comprehensive index and bibliography.

Among many who have helped me with information on some particular aspect of the history I would like to mention: Professor

Peter Hall; the Registrar of Charterhouse; Mr G. C. Berry of the Metropolitan Water Board; Mr Duncan Grant; Miss Baslington of the Methodist Archives; Mr Douglas Craig, Administrator of Sadler's Wells Theatre; Miss D. Rait Kerr, Curator of the M.C.C.; Lieutenant-Colonel P. Massey, Secretary of the Honourable Artillery Company; the Curator of St John of Jerusalem; Miss Carpenter, of Dame Alice Owen's Girls' School; Mr John Croydon; Mr Roy Drew; Professor Barrie Scott; the Reverend Peter Johnston.

In conclusion I would like to thank Miss G. Kuehl for typing my manuscript with so much care and attention to detail.

P. Z.

PICTURE ACKNOWLEDGEMENTS

WE are grateful to the following for permission to use the photographs listed below:
Vera Skinner for plate 30
The Press Association for plate 50
The Keystone Press for plate 45
G. R. Taylor for plate 25
The Metropolitan Water Board for plate 18
The Greater London Council for plates 26, 36, 37 and 39
Jerry Mason for plates 32, 35, 40, 41, 44 and 49
Islington Libraries for plates 1, 2, 3, 4, 5, 6, 7, 8, 9, 10, 11, 12, 13, 14, 15, 16, 17, 19, 20, 21, 22, 23, 27, 28, 29, 31, 33, 34, 38, 42, 46, 47 and 48
And to the Islington Council and H.M. Stationery Office for the map of Islington

Contents

Illustrations

Introduction

ISLINGTON, one of the inner boroughs of London, consists of the historic areas of Barnsbury, Canonbury, Clerkenwell, Finsbury, Highbury, Holloway and St Peter's.

To the east of Islington the flatness of Hackney and Stoke Newington stretches away to form the old cockney East End; and to the south is the historic commercial centre of London, the City. To the north, Islington merges into suburban North London at the foot of Highgate Hill; and to the west is Camden, an area as varied and heterogeneous as Islington. Hampstead Heath, one of London's largest open spaces, and the theatres and shops of the West End are now within half-an-hour's car journey of Islington.

Parts of Islington still show traces of the mass poverty of Edwardian and Victorian England. Others have achieved a degree of opulence which they have never known before. Cheek by jowl with interiors richly decorated in current trends and furnished with expensive antique or modern furniture are rooms in the same terraces which have been neither decorated nor modernized for decades. This essentially modern urban district is a mixture of many classes and races who have transformed the many architectural styles to suit their particular style of living.

The effect of a rich and continuous history since medieval times is still discernible in the street patterns and buildings of Islington. The development of the borough was often affected by great events such as the Great Fire of London; yet Islington, with its tea-gardens and music halls, its markets and prisons, its religious foundations and schools, had a fascinating past of its own.

DERIVATION OF ISLINGTON

The first known reference to 'Islington' is found in A.D. 1000. Traditionally, however, the Romans had camps in Highbury and Barnsbury and Boadicea is said to have fought her last battle against Suetonious Paulinus near King's Cross in A.D. 61. Then, *Gislandune*, which means 'Gisla's hill or down', is mentioned in an Anglo-Saxon charter. Skinner, the historian of London, suggested in 1796 that *Iseldon*, as it became, is derived from the Anglo-Saxon *Gisel*, a hostage, and *dune*, a hill, town, or fort, indicating that hostages were held here. Hughson, the historian, stated in 1809 that Islington was derived from *Ishel* meaning lower, and *don* (or *twyn*) meaning a fortified enclosure. The Domesday Book (*c.* 1086) refers to the hamlet in the Great Forest of Middlesex as *Isendone*. The canons of St Paul's held most of the land, part of which was arable or pasture serving the cattle of the village. Rannulf, who is described as the brother of Ilger, possessed arable and pasture land at *Tolentone* (later part of the manor of Highbury) and 'pannage for sixty hogs', indicating the forest which then existed.

RELIGIOUS FOUNDATIONS IN FINSBURY

In the twelfth century the Benedictine nuns and the Knights of St John established their foundations in Finsbury on land given to them by Jordan de Briset. Finsbury was not mentioned in the Domesday Book – some suppose that it was part of Islington then; others that the land was held by the Crown. The religious foundations were probably attracted by the good water supplies from wells and streams in this part of Islington just north of the City. Fitzstephen, a monk, commented in about 1180 that there were 'fields for pasture and open meadows, very pleasant, into which the river waters do flow, and mills are turned about with a delightful noise. The arable lands are no hungry pieces of gravel ground, but like the rich fields of Asia, which plentifully bring forth corn and fill the barn of the owner with a dainty crop of the fruit of Ceres. Beyond them an immense forest extends itself, beautified with woods and groves, and full of the lairs and coverts of wild beasts and game, stags, bucks, bears and wild bulls.'

FEUDAL MANORS IN ISLINGTON

Shortly before the death of Ralph de Berners in 1297, the manor of Barnsbury which he then held was described as consisting mainly of corn-land, with a very small part being meadow. Barnsbury, which he also held under the Bishop of London in return for a certain quit-rent and the service of warding Stortford Castle, was one of six manors which made up Islington in feudal times. The Prebend manor had been restored to the Canons of St Paul in about 1065. The manor of Canonbury was granted to the priory of St Bartholomew's, Smithfield, in 1253 by Ralph de Berners, and the manor of Highbury was given to the Knights of St John of Jerusalem in 1271 by Alicia de Barowe. These four manors are indicated in the Domesday Book; that of St John of Jerusalem grew as various landholders donated land in Clerkenwell, Islington proper and Hornsey; and the manor of Clerkenwell, which took its name from the parish of Clerkenwell, consisted of land situated in Upper Holloway.

PLEASURE GROUNDS FOR LONDONERS

Until the eighteenth century the fields of Islington provided one of the nearest pleasure grounds for Londoners. Stow, the historian, says the fields to the north of London were 'commodious for the citizens therein to walke, shoote, and otherwise to recreate and refresh their dulled spirits, in the sweet and wholesome ayre'.

Archery

Henry VIII encouraged the sport of archery to the extent of making it a father's duty to provide a bow and two arrows for his son at the age of seven, and compelling all but clergy and judges to exercise at the 'butts'. These marks were stones or posts of different heights set at distances from 180 to 380 yards apart, providing a golf-like course for the archers to practise their shots; they numbered about 160 in Finsbury alone in the early seventeenth century. Both James I and Charles I thought the butts so important that they issued edicts to stop the fields being enclosed, which would 'interrupt the necessary and profitable exercise of shooting'.

Champion archers were ennobled by Henry VIII in sporting jest after a shooting match at Windsor with titles such as the 'Duke of Shoreditch' and the 'Marquess of Islington'. The farmers and cowkeepers in Islington had to put up with whizzing arrows and cocky archers until the eighteenth century when they managed to have the butts removed; the members of the Honourable Artillery Company, however, made one unfortunate cowkeeper named Pitfield renew a butt in 1746 which was inscribed 'Pitfield's Repentance'. Dame Alice Owen narrowly missed being injured by an arrow as a child; she was so overjoyed at her escape that in 1613 she built a school and almshouses on the spot facing St John's Street, at that time a main thoroughfare from the City.

Duck-Hunting

In the sixteenth century the ponds of Islington provided much sport for those who came duck-hunting with their dogs. Ben Jonson referred to the 'citizens that come a-ducking to Islington ponds' in his comedy *Every Man in his Humour*. Sir William D'Avenant, who succeeded Ben Jonson as poet-laureate, must have enjoyed this townsman's version of beagling many a time for he wrote:

> *Ho! Ho! – to Islington – enough –*
> *Fetch Job my son, and our dog Ruffe;*
> *For there, in pond, through mire and muck,*
> *We'll cry, hay, duck – there Ruffe – hay, duck.*

One pond close to Newington Green eventually took the name of a certain John Ball, who owned a nearby house of entertainment; this keeper is still remembered in Ball's Pond Road. The reservoir of the New River Head was, according to Edmund Howes, author of *Chronicles*, 'in former times an open idell pool, commonly called The Ducking Pond'. The White Conduit had its Wheel Pond used for duck-hunting, and some land near Liverpool Road was known as the Ducking Pond Field. By the middle of the seventeenth century the popularity of duck-hunting in Islington seems to have waned as the ponds – and probably the ducks – disappeared. In the spring of 1664 Samuel Pepys, the son of a London tailor, noted in his diary: 'Thence walked through the ducking-pond fields; but they are so altered since my father used to carry us to Islington, to the old man's, at the King's Head, to eat cakes and ale (his name was Pitts), that I did not know which was the ducking-pond, nor where I was.'

ELIZABETHAN VILLAGE

In Elizabethan times Islington proper (excluding Finsbury) was a large village with parish church, a green, and with country mansions and other houses situated between the Upper Street and Lower Street, though by that time the Elizabethans probably regarded it as a town. John Strype (1643–1737), the English historical writer, described Islington as 'a country town . . . so pleasantly seated' when Queen Elizabeth attempted to visit it in 1581, but on this occasion she had to turn back as she was besieged by beggars. At various times her favourites, Sir Walter Raleigh, the Earl of Leicester and the Earl of Essex, are said to have resided in Islington. The manor house of the Knights of St John of Jerusalem in Highbury, destroyed in 1381, was in little more than ruins at that time, but Canonbury House, where the Canons of St Bartholomew had had their country retreat, remained; this was transformed into a magnificent mansion of its period by Sir John Spencer, sometime Lord Mayor of London. Nearby stood the house of Sir Thomas Fowler, a juror at the trial of Sir Walter Raleigh. The Queen was said to have visited Islington frequently; she was certainly entertained in Finsbury by the Duke of Norfolk in the Charterhouse; he had turned the fourteenth-century monastery into a fine mansion. At the Reformation, the Benedictine nunnery and the priory of St John in Finsbury had been dissolved, but the latter was used by the Queen's Master of Revels, Edmund Tylney, for rehearsals for court entertainments. Despite Elizabeth's proclamation in 1580 prohibiting the building of any new houses within three miles of the City gates, Islington and Finsbury obviously continued to grow, because in 1656 it was necessary to pass an Act of Parliament preventing building within *ten* miles of the city!

CLERKENWELL AFTER THE FIRE OF LONDON

Towards the end of the seventeenth century Clerkenwell, with its parish church and green, became a fashionable village. The Duke of Newcastle moved here to live on the site of the nunnery.

Refugees from the Plague and the Great Fire of London in the 1660s moved out to the north of the City. John Evelyn, the diarist, commented that they dispersed as far as Highgate, 'some under miserable tents and hovels, many without a rag or any necessary utensils, bed, or board, who from delicateness, riches, and easy accommodations in stately and well-furnished houses, were now reduced to extremest misery and poverty . . . I then went towards Islington and Highgate, where one might have seen 200,000 people, of all ranks and degrees, dispersed and lying along by their heaps of what they could save from the fire, deploring their loss, and though ready to perish for hunger and destitution, yet not asking one penny for relief, which to me appeared a stranger sight than any I had yet beheld.'

Within the next few decades the number of houses in the parish of Clerkenwell trebled and the new adjoining parish of St Luke's, formed in 1733, was, as Lewis, the historian of Islington, states, 'laid out in numerous streets and squares, covered with buildings in every direction, and has become one of the most extensive and populous parishes in the suburbs of the metropolis'.

TEA-GARDENS OF THE EIGHTEENTH CENTURY

To the north of Clerkenwell, most of Islington's tea-gardens were concentrated in the fields surrounding the New River Head, which had supplied the City with water since 1613. These tea-gardens blossomed round the rediscovered springs, and attracted City-dwellers with their artificial rurality and variety of entertainment. In the fourteenth century the wells in this district had provided a backcloth for the clerks from the City to perform their mystery plays; in 1409 'most part of the nobles and gentles in England', according to Stow, were lured to see a play at the Skinners' well which lasted eight days. Mr Sadler drew the crowds from 1684 to see his wells, and contortionists and acrobats were provided by him for their amusement. The owner of Islington Spa opposite was quick to trade on the society yearnings to take the waters which he advertised as the 'New Tunbridge Wells'; society, and others, revelled there, much to the chagrin of the spa-owners at Tunbridge! White Conduit House and

Dobney's on the crest of Pentonville Hill had fine views in their early days. The loaves of White Conduit that were hawked through the London streets were an advertisement no tea-garden in Islington would seem to have bettered. Oliver Goldsmith, who enjoyed many of his 'day-tripper' jaunts there, wrote in *The Citizen of the World*: 'Here the inhabitants of London often assemble to celebrate a feast of hot rolls and butter; seeing such numbers, each with their little tables before them, employed on this occasion, must no doubt be a very amusing sight to the looker-on, but still more so to those who perform the solemnity.' Dobney's, like its rival the Three Hats, laid on feats of horsemanship which most circus-goers would marvel at today. Bull-baiting, promenading, cricketing, bowling, dancing, eating and drinking, were all part of the pleasures Londoners sought in the open country within tramping distance of the City. Some of the amusement gardens, such as Copenhagen House and Merlin's Cave, are echoed in street names; but Highbury Barn, the Barley Mow, the English Grotto, the Pantheon, and others, all had their appeal – much like fun-fairs today.

LONDON'S DAIRY

Although the nurseries and market gardens supplied London with their produce, Islington was really London's dairy. In the eighteenth century Holloway cheesecakes were as famous as Chelsea buns, and were hawked through the streets by men on horseback. As late as the turn of the century, Mr William Vaughan, then a boy in Finsbury, recalls that 'of the street sights and sounds of my boyhood days, there were many which seem quaint; for instance I always fetched the morning milk from Little Sutton Street in which a cow stood eating hay from the ground, while the animal was milked, and sold to people waiting with their jugs and cans, at 1½d. a pint.' Samuel Lewis recorded in 1842: 'The land in the neighbourhood of Islington is principally occupied by cowkeepers, who have very extensive dairies for supplying the inhabitants of the metropolis with milk; but the trade of the place chiefly depends on the resident population.'

Among the more prosperous farmers was Mr Samuel Rhodes, great-grandfather of Cecil Rhodes, the South African statesman. In the 1820s he kept between four and six hundred cows among which Nelson (another of Islington's historians) said were to be seen 'the finest specimens of large and handsome cattle in the environs of the metropolis, or, perhaps in the whole kingdom'. These cows were fed with local hay stacked near the south end of Colebrooke Terrace. Mr Richard Laycock had a large dairy farm in Barnsbury and some of his cow-lairs remained in the street named after him until the 1890s. His cows, as the historian Cromwell reported in 1834, averaged nine quarts a day, and the milk was taken from the cow-house to be sold mainly by robust Welsh girls and Irish women. 'It is amazing', Cromwell stated, 'to witness the fatigue these females undergo, and the hilarity and cheerfulness that prevail among them, and which tend so greatly to lighten their very laborious employment. Even in the most inclement weather, and in the depth of winter, they arrive here in parties from different parts of the metropolis by three or four o'clock in the morning, laughing and singing to the music of their empty pails: with these, when filled, they return to town; and the weight they are thus accustomed to carry on their yokes, for the distance of several miles, is sometimes from 100 to 130 pounds.'

VICTORIAN BUILDING

Builders and speculators soon turned the hay-making fields of Islington into a quagmire of roads and brickfields. In Islington proper, imposing terraces such as Highbury Terrace with its fine views over fields, or Colebrooke Row with its outlook on the New River, were built in the second half of the eighteenth century. New parish churches replaced older ones: St Mary's, Islington, in 1754, and St James's, Clerkenwell, in 1792. The industrious Victorians, spurred on first by better roads, and later by better transport, turned the fields into streets and squares, terraces and villas, churches and prisons, and little remained for parks. Their legacy left city-dwellers richer but users of open spaces poorer: to this day Islington is one of the most impoverished London boroughs when it comes to open space. Highbury Fields and the linear New River Walk remain exceptional 'islands of solitude' (in Macaulay's words) where very rarely, if indeed at all, may still be enjoyed the silence and repose of the country area Islington once was.

LONDON going out of Town. — or — The March of Bricks & Mortar.

Cartoon by George Cruikshank, 1 November 1829

The air at Islington was considered so good towards the end of the eighteenth century that it was known as the 'London hospital'. Nelson tells how an old woman declining in health came to Islington on the advice of her doctor. She agreed to take a suite of rooms on condition that the banisters, which were in disrepair, were mended. 'Madam,' replied the landlady, 'that will answer no purpose, as the undertakers' men, in bringing down the coffins, are continually breaking the banisters.'

Public Buildings

In the mid-nineteenth century the farmers were lured from the country to show and trade their cattle at the vast Caledonian market opened by Prince Albert, and at the Agricultural Hall, where the first show was attended by the Prince of Wales. Penton-ville and Holloway prisons, the fortress-like monuments to Victorian enlightenment, remain intact, but no longer isolated from the community by fields. Many of the huge churches – the pride of Victorian congregations – are decaying or have been demolished; and the athenaeums no longer exist.

Islington Green

In 1864 Mr Sam Collins turned the Lansdowne Arms on Islington Green into his own 'chapel-on-the-green' music hall, and in 1891 at the Grand Theatre opposite the Angel, Lottie Collins appeared as Alice in *Dick Whittington*. These theatres have gone, but for a few years there has been a plan to create a Globe-type theatre in St George's Church, Tufnell Park. At Islington Green, Mr Gladstone, Chancellor of the Exchequer at the time, unveiled a statue in 1862 to one of Islington's greatest (if not *the* greatest) entrepreneurs: Sir Hugh Myddelton, who in 1613 brought water supplies for the City to the New River Head in Rosebery Avenue.

COACH ROUTE TO THE NORTH

Many of the inns along Upper Street and Holloway Road served the coach trade, at a time when fresh horses and a bed for the night were at a premium. Between 1812 and 1840 the engraver James Pollard recorded his rich impressions of stylized coaches drawn by clockwork-like horses and brimming with excited passengers. Pollard knew the scene well as he had been born at Spa Fields in 1792 and his father, an engraver in Holloway, published his first prints. At the Peacock, which stood near the Angel, the northbound mail coaches from the old General Post Office in Lombard Street would stop to pick up passengers who had come from the West End. Here, as described by Thomas Hughes in *Tom Brown's Schooldays*, Tom and his father spent a short night before the Tally-Ho for Rugby arrived. There was much competition between rival owners of these fast coaches and Pollard showed two of them driving neck and neck past the Crown in Holloway, with that of Mrs Mountain (who had introduced the first Tally-Ho between London and Birmingham) having the edge. But with the coming of the railways, Pollard was reduced to painting omnibuses, such as those which left the Nag's Head for the City.

Of these inns, the Angel at Islington was undoubtedly, for its day, the terminal with most character. Mr Noah Claypole, who walked past the inn with Charlotte in Dickens's *Oliver Twist*, wisely judged, from the crowd of passengers and number of vehicles, that here London began in earnest. Until 1819 the building looked like a large old country inn, with two rows of windows in a long frontage, topped with an overhanging roof. In the quadrangle yard of the Elizabethan-style inn, strolling players performed for the groundlings while the double galleries were crowded with more fortunate spectators. Until the 1780s travellers would stay the night at the Angel rather than risk the roads and threat of footpads beyond. Farmers and graziers on their way to Smithfield market made the Angel their 'peculiar resort'. Thomas Paine, the radical thinker who took part in the American and French revolutions, is said to have written *The Rights of Man* (published in 1792) at the Angel, though others claim it was at the Old Red Lion in St John Street. In the 1820s James Pollard painted some of the royal mail coaches outside the Angel when they celebrated the King's birthday procession.

The inn took its name from the angel who appeared before the Virgin Mary at the annunciation with a scroll in his hands in medieval tradition inscribed: 'Ave Maria, gratia plena, Dominus tecum'. After the Reformation this original sign was thought too Popish and so Mary was left out and the angel appeared alone. Ironically, the Angel is in Finsbury and not in Islington proper. Thomas Coull tells the story of a pauper who, having died on the corner of Liverpool Road, was buried by Clerkenwell after the Islington authorities had refused their permission. As a result Clerkenwell claimed that piece of land as part of its parish, though Islington retained the land facing the Angel as far as the City Road on the other side of the High Street. The traffic intersection is dominated nowadays by a former Lyons Corner House; the brownish building with its frieze of angel faces peering down is topped by an ornamental cupola at the corner. The turn-of-the-century design, in Pevsner's words, 'of jolly commercial vulgarity', is by Eedle and Meyers.

The name of the Angel is now more important as an underground station on the Northern line. For many years there have been schemes for redeveloping the Angel area, but the question of what should be done remains more complex than any game of Monopoly. The problem is one of maintaining traffic flow at these major crossroads without destroying the character peculiar to this heart of Islington.

VICTORIAN MIGRATION

The migration of the middle classes from the area in Victorian times seems to have taken place much earlier in Finsbury than in Islington. In 1885 the Reverend William Dawson, Rector of St John's, Clerkenwell, wrote: 'Within the time covered by Her Majesty's "happy reign", merchants, lawyers, doctors, wealthy watchmakers and jewellers [the watchmaking and jewellery trade was long the staple trade of Clerkenwell] lived in Red Lion Street and St John's Square, and kept their carriages in the adjacent mews. Early in the present reign a movement set in towards the suburbs. It was easy for such people to have their houses and gardens a few miles northwards, at Highbury, Hampstead or Highgate, and drive daily into business. Presently the tradespeople followed their example. The houses thus emptied were let out in tenements, and were largely occupied by working jewellers, compositors, and printers.' The Medical Officer in Clerkenwell confirmed this trend in 1881 with the comment that 'there are some good houses, where some good families were brought up, where they used to keep their carriages; they retire into the country, and those houses are let to a family in each floor, there is a continual outgo of good people, and an in-come of working people'.

TWENTIETH-CENTURY DECLINE

In Islington proper the middle classes seem to have moved out mainly in the 1880s and the 1890s. Charles Booth – who based the researches for his 'Poverty map' on the knowledge of local school-board visitors and policemen – shows that by the 1890s most of the well-to-do had moved from Barnsbury, though they still dominated Canonbury and Tufnell Park. In Highbury, as the map in his *Life and Labour in London* (1902) indicates, the large villas in Highbury Hill, Highbury New Park and Aberdeen Park were still kept by the wealthy with many servants and carriages. No doubt some patronized the military tournament at the Royal Agricultural Hall, considered part of the London season in the 1890s. But by the time Edward VII was king, they had moved, though optimistic estate agents (hoping for their return) were offering the houses free to anyone who would maintain their gardens! By the 'twenties the fashionable homes of the affluent Victorians had become boarding-houses, offices and warehouses; the centre of Milner Square was a vegetable garden and Thornhill Square had seen better days, as the Royal Commission on Squares noted in 1927. The houses no longer had postal addresses with the right ring: Thomas Burke, in his novel *The Sun in Splendour* (1927), described them thus: 'The basements with barred windows, the area bells, the stone steps and the porticoes, all whisper of prosperity; but the basements are self-contained flats or little warehouses, and four families sleep in the four floors that once were the pride of mistresses and the penalty of maids. They are like old musical boxes that have stopped dead in the middle of the air . . . They endure in their long downfall, spreading around them a spirit of melancholy and decay. Theirs is not the tragic fall from grandeur; they have only slipped from the middle-class to the lower-middle-class.' This was borne out by the *New Survey of London Life and Labour* conducted by the London School of Economics in 1931, which put forward the theory that the higher the ground on which the houses were built, the higher the social character seemed to be; a contrast was drawn between the hills of Highbury, Canonbury, Holloway and Tufnell Park and the south-western slopes of the then Islington borough.

OVERCROWDING IN ISLINGTON

As Islington became overcrowded, and more industries and enterprises established themselves in the neighbourhood, the middle classes migrated to find better neighbours elsewhere. The railways opened up suburbs for both middle and working classes, though until the turn of the century, much of the northern part of Islington was still being built.

There were two crises of overcrowding: the first was in the 1850s as vast areas such as Somers Town were demolished to make way for the railways and their terminals in central London. Consequently adjoining areas, such as Islington, became even more overcrowded as displaced residents moved to stay near their work. In 1865 Dr Edward Ballard, the medical officer, commented that in the parish of St Mary's there was 'an excess of Law Clerks, Commercial Clerks, Schoolmasters, Printers, Goldsmiths, Jewellers, Watchmakers, Butchers, Carpenters and Joiners, Bricklayers, Plasterers and Brickmakers. In the remaining five we stand more or less below London generally as to number, namely, Publicans, Bakers, Tailors, Shoemakers and Labourers. In the case of Females, we have a slight excess of Schoolmistresses, Dressmakers and Milliners, Washerwomen and Domestic Servants.'

The second crisis of overcrowding was largely due to the failure of the Artisans' Dwelling Act of 1875. Under this act, the authorities were, for the first time, empowered to carry out an extensive slum-clearance programme in order to rehouse slum-dwellers in proper 'dwellings'. But ironically, as Gareth Stedman Jones has pointed out, instead of alleviating overcrowding, this act intensified the problem. Those who took their cut were the owners of the slum properties which the Metropolitan Board of Works took over, and the middle men or 'house knackers' who, for instance on the Marquess of Northampton's estate in Clerkenwell, found it more profitable to let a house off in single rooms to working-class tenants than as a whole house to middle-class tenants. The displaced poor crowded into tenements wherever they could, as the workmen's dwellings provided under the act had rules which in many cases excluded them.

As the well-to-do moved out, more workshops, offices and warehouses moved to become neighbours to former town houses; in Barnsbury, for instance, the Congregational chapel on the corner of Milner Square became an iron foundry. After the introduction of the Cheap Trains Act of 1883, suburbs were built for workmen as well as for the well-to-do; and these no doubt contributed to the decline in population in Islington proper in the twentieth century.

Decline in Population

Although there had been a decline in the population in Finsbury since 1861 and in Islington after 1901, the whole of Islington is today one of the most densely populated boroughs in London. In 1970 there were 61·8 persons per acre, compared with the Greater London average of 19·3. The total population now is less than the estimated crowd of a quarter of a million which turned out to cheer the Arsenal football team through the streets of Islington after they won the double in 1971. For this triumph, Islington's own team was honoured with the Freedom of the Borough.

These are the population figures from census returns:

Year	Islington	Finsbury
1801	10,212	55,515
1821	22,417	86,223
1841	55,690	112,986
1861	155,341	129,073
1871	216,000	124,766
1881	283,000	119,409
1891	319,000	111,543
1901	335,238	101,463
1911	327,403	87,923
1921	330,737	75,995
1931	321,795	69,888
1941	182,910 (est.)	(1938 est. 56,960)
1951	235,632	35,620
1961	228,833	33,020
1971	estimate 200,730 (for both)	

POSTWAR RETURN OF THE MIDDLE CLASSES

After the Second World War the middle classes returned to Islington to houses which were once elegant, but now, more often than not, were endowed with Victorian plumbing hardly suited for modern living. In the 1930s, parts such as Canonbury had been the haven of academics and artists who found Islington conveniently central and inexpensive. In the 1960s journalists, architects, lawyers, accountants, teachers and designers were attracted by the character of the Regency and Victorian terraces and squares; paradoxically their very deterioration had preserved them from additions, alterations or demolition for decades. Their interiors have been transformed; some, such as Max Clendinning's house in Alwyne Road, influenced modern trends. Margaret Drabble, the novelist, who lived in Highbury during the 1960s, describes a visit of Clara, the heroine, in *Jerusalem the Golden:* 'As they drew nearer to Gabriel's house, they crossed a couple of squares with which Clara was vaguely familiar, squares once thoroughly decayed, and now full of that apparatus of demolition and construction; the area attracted her strongly, in its violent seedy contrasts, its juxtaposition of the rich and the poor, its rejection of suburban uniformity. Anything unfamiliar attracted her . . . She looked at the peeling, cracked facades, and the newly-plastered, smartly painted ones, and she thought that she would like to have lived there, among such new examples.'

LOCAL GOVERNMENT

With the turn of the century local government passed from the vestries to elected councils; Clerkenwell vestry hall in Rosebery Avenue became the Finsbury town hall, while in Islington, then a separate borough, a new town hall was built in Upper Street in 1925. As the councils took increasing responsibility for better subsidized housing in the decades following, more and more of the charitable workmen's dwellings, thought solid enough in Victorian times, were to disappear.

By the 1960s Sir Milner Holland found that Islington and Finsbury were among the areas of greatest housing stress in Greater London. Postwar slum-clearance programmes led to controversies such as those concerning the Packington estate and the Barnsbury experimental traffic scheme.

COAT OF ARMS

In 1965 Islington became one of the largest London boroughs with a total area of 3,678·6 acres when it absorbed Finsbury, which, however, still retains its peculiar character. After the next general election in the mid-'seventies the borough will be represented in Parliament by three members, for Islington North, Islington Central, and Islington South and Finsbury respectively. In the council's coat of arms some of the rich associations of Islington's past may be traced. The Berners family who owned the manor of Yseldon in the thirteenth century contribute the water-bouget from its arms; and the arrow symbolizes the once popular sport of archery. The yellow crescent and rings are from the arms of Sir Thomas Sutton, founder of the seventeenth-century Charterhouse, and the rings also occur in the arms of Sir Richard Whittington, who traditionally turned back at the foot of Highgate Hill to become Lord Mayor of London. The blue and white waves suggest the part played by water in Islington's history through the development of the New River and the wells of Finsbury. The book of learning represents the educational institutions associated with the borough, such as the City University and the Polytechnic of North London. The Maltese Cross is that of the Order of St John of Jerusalem, whose Knights Hospitallers founded the priory in Finsbury. For a borough which throughout its history has served London well, providing its citizens with sport, entertainment, industry and houses, it is appropriate that the motto of the enlarged council is simply 'We Serve'.

B

I

Finsbury: Bunhill

Finsbury (which now forms the southern part of Islington) takes its name from the family of Finnes, also spelt Fynes, or Fiennes. This family owned land north of the City and, traditionally, gave part of Moorfields to the City in trust for the use of its citizens. The manor house of Finsbury stood north of the Moorgate and is clearly shown in 1559 on the earliest known map of London – a four-square house with its great barn, gatehouse and stables, court and orchard. In the thirteenth and fourteenth centuries there is mention of Finsbury in the form of Vinisbir and Vynesburi.

Until the sixteenth century Moorfields was 'a waste and unprofitable ground', too soft and spongy for building and cultivation. At wintertime, the 'great fen, or moor which watereth the walls of the City on the north side' became a skating ground for citizens, as Fitzstephen, the twelfth-century monk, indicates. In 1415 the Moorgate was built in the City walls for 'the citizens to walk that way upon causeys towards Iseldon and Hoxton', and by 1527 the moor had been properly drained. The common fields became so popular with archers and walkers that they demonstrated against their enclosure by taking up shovels and spades to level the hedges and fill up the ditches! Laundresses would dry their washing in the fields; and playgoers would make their way along the paved moat-bank, still known as Finsbury Pavement, to theatres such as the Fortune, built in 1599 near Golden Lane for Edward Alleyn, the founder of Dulwich College. A plaque in Fortune Street records the site. Shakespeare in *Henry IV: Part I* gives an inkling of how popular the fields were

The New Artillery Ground and Moorfields in 1732

with those living in the City. Hotspur mentions Finsbury in the following lines to his wife:

> *And giv'st such sarcenet surety for thy oaths,*
> *As if thou never walk'dst further than Finsbury.*

Stow, the English chronicler, writing towards the end of the sixteenth century, noted the increase in summer-houses, 'some of them like Midsummer pageants, with towers, turrets and chimney-tops, not so much for use of profit as for show and pleasure, betraying the vanity of men's minds'.

Bunhill, which forms the south-east part of the area of Finsbury, derives its name from a prehistoric burial ground known as Bone Hill. After the devastation of the Black Death in 1348, Sir Walter de Manny founded the Charterhouse for the Carthusian order on sixteen acres – some of which had served as burial grounds for victims of the plague. During the sixteenth century, after the marshes of Moorfields were drained, the Honourable Artillery Company established its parade ground to the east of Bunhill Row.

Whitefield preaching in Moorfields in 1742

In the seventeenth and eighteenth centuries, Moorfields was popular with nonconformists; the Wesleys, and Whitefield, preached in the open air to the crowds, and streets bearing names such as 'Worship' and 'Tabernacle' indicate the nonconformist influence in the area. The first Wesleyan chapel was built nearby in City Road and to the west Bunhill Fields was used as a burial ground by the dissenters from 1665 until 1852.

CHARACTER

Bunhill is still strong in its nonconformist associations – the Wesleyan mother church in City Road and the burial ground of Bunhill Fields remain. The parade ground of the Honourable Artillery Company offers a glimpse of the open meadows that Moorfields once was. The former parish of St Luke's, formed in the seventeenth century, is now dominated by modern council housing and Finsbury Square, once a fine eighteenth-century square, is now very much part of the City with its commercial buildings. The fine Tudor mansion of Charterhouse, built on the site of the fourteenth-century monastery, although not in the modern ward of Bunhill but in the adjoining Clerkenwell, is dealt with in this chapter. In 1965 the borough of Finsbury (with its three wards of Pentonville, Clerkenwell and Bunhill) became part of the enlarged borough of Islington. To the south lies the City; Holborn to the west; Islington proper to the north; and Hackney to the east.

MOORFIELDS

Just to the north of Finsbury Street through ornamental iron gates lies the parade ground of the Honourable Artillery Company where pikemen drilled and archers practised after their move here in 1641 from the Old Artillery Garden off Bishopsgate. This green, once part of the open country, now hemmed in with houses along its boundaries, still conveys a strong impression of the country. Chiswell Street was flanked with water-courses with bridges across it into the fields. From 1737 to 1909 the foundry established by William Caslon, well-known for his graceful 'old face' type, stood in Chiswell Street, as a blue plaque now shows.

SAMUEL WHITBREAD'S BREWERY

Samuel Whitbread moved his brewery to a little brewhouse on the south side of Chiswell Street in 1750: to the west of the arch into the brewery yard can be seen the front door of the Partners' Dwelling House where he lived. In 1774 he added the Porter Tun Room to the brewing buildings. The Cinderella-like golden coach of the Lord Mayor is housed here, and each year in November it takes part in his procession through the City; six grey shires draw the coach, which is attended by the draymen (who deliver the beer which is still brewed here) as coachmen, postillions and walking grooms, splendid in their colourful livery.

THE HONOURABLE ARTILLERY COMPANY

When the Artillery Company moved to its 'new artillery garden' its neighbours in Bunhill Row protested that the high brick boundary wall would turn the pleasant passage into a noisome lane and they would be forced to hire a scavenger to clean it! In the 1670s John Milton, the poet, spent his last days with his third wife, Elizabeth Minshull, in Artillery Walk, as it was known. By then, the members of the Honourable Artillery Company had shown their courage and discipline in the Civil War from 1642 to 1646. They became a force on which Parliament relied in every emergency. Sir Charles Firth noted that 'without their aid, Essex could not have relieved Gloucester, nor could Waller have repulsed Hopton's invasion of Sussex. They were not very well disciplined, and were too accustomed to good food and good beds to support with patience the hardships of a campaign, but they were well drilled'. The Earl of Clarendon, however, formed a different impression of their discipline at Newbury – he wrote that 'when their wings of horse were scattered and dispersed, [they] kept their ground so steadily, that though Prince Rupert himself led up the choice horse to charge them, and endured their storm of small shot, he could make no impression upon their stand of pikes, but was forced to wheel about; of so sovereign benefit is that readiness, order and dexterity in the use of their arms, which hath been so much neglected'.

FINSBURY ARCHER'S TICKET FOR THE SHOOTING OF 1676.

" All Gentlemen, Lovers of the noble Society of Archery, are desired to meet
Drapers Hall in *Throgmorton-street*, on Monday the 24*th* day of *July*, 1676,
Twelve of the Clock precisely ; and according to ancient custom of *Finsbury*
chers, to deliver to the Bearer hereof Mr. *William Wood*, upon receipt of
s Ticket, Two Shillings and Six pence, that Provision may be made accor-
gly. This serves also to give notice, That the Elevenscore Target shall be
up by us in the *New-Artillery*-Ground, upon Wednesday the 26*th* day of
y following ; and that day to begin to shoot at the same, by Nine of the Clock
it was begun and shot at the last year). All Archers intending to shoot at
same, are to pay down their Twenty Shillings upon the 24*th* day of *July*,
to us, or either of us, or to Mr. *William Wood*, that Plate may be provided,
l further trouble prevented of sending to Archers for the same ; the place

Armoury House

Nowadays, the members of the oldest armed force in the country, now part of the reserve army, meet and drill in their spare time, in the Armoury House and on the green which this building (dating from 1735) overlooks. The atmosphere within is much like that of a London club – from the panelled first-floor mess the members look out on fields where cricket is still played and from where, in 1784, Mr Lunardi made the first manned balloon flight in Britain accompanied by a dog, a cat and a pigeon! Since the Civil War, monarchs have been careful to see that the Captain-General of the company, if not the Sovereign himself, was at least the Prince of Wales or Prince Consort! Their portraits hang in the Armoury House, together with one of Mr Edward Heath, the present Prime Minister, who was Lieutenant-Colonel commanding the 2nd regiment from 1947 to 1951. The company forms a guard

Artillery Barracks, City Road

of honour whenever the monarch visits the City and has the privilege of marching through the City with drums beating, colours flying and bayonets fixed.

In 1537 Henry VIII incorporated the members of the Guild of St George, who had practised their archery near Bishopsgate, as the 'Guylde of Artillary of Longbowes, Crosbowes and Handegonnes'. These archers established their practising butts in the fields of Finsbury and Islington; a map of the shooting butts, together with a stone archery mark dubbed 'Scarlet', is now in Armoury House. In 1708, Edward Hatton, in *A New View of London*, observed, 'They do by prescription march over all the ground from the Artillery Ground to Islington . . . breaking down gates etc, that obstructed them in such marches.' During the Gordon riots of 1780, the company defended the nearby Bank of England. By 1857 'heroic' barracks designed by Jennings in the form of a turreted castle were built facing the City Road. In the Armoury House is a fine collection of arms from the various battles in which the company has fought. In the Court Room, with its associations of George I, is a copy of the Great Vellum Book, which contains signatures of many illustrious members; among them were the first Duke of Marlborough, the first Duke of Albemarle, Samuel Pepys and Christopher Wren.

FINSBURY SQUARE

Finsbury Square, once a fine Georgian square, was built from 1777 onwards; nowadays there is little of the elegance left which so attracted doctors of Harley Street standing. Among the residents was Dr George Birkbeck (1776–1841) who in 1824 did much to found the London Mechanics or Birkbeck Institute, later to become part of the University of London. Dr David Livingstone, the Scottish missionary, stayed in the square for a short time in 1856. Dr Nathan Adler (1803–90), the Chief Rabbi, who lived in the square founded the Jews' College there in 1855 where it remained until 1958.

The square, laid out by George Dance the younger and designed by J. Peacock, has been displaced by twentieth-century office buildings; of these, Royal London House by J. J. Joass, with its jagged tower, is, in Pevsner's words, the most 'victoriously vulgar'.

WESLEY'S CHAPEL

The plainness of the front of Wesley's chapel, set back from the City Road like a country house, belies its importance to Methodists the world over.

In 1777 John Wesley pushed his way through the crowd on a stormy day to lay the foundation stone of the new chapel, which

Wesley's original foundry

THE FOUNDERY.

A Mr Wesley's Apartments
B Mr Wesley's Study
C Bell rung at 5 o'Clock to Morning Service
   at 9 Evening Family Prayer, & sundry other times
D Common Entrance to all parts of the premises
   also to Public Service in the Chapel

E Entrance to Chapel only
F Dwelling House for the family preachers
   &c. entrance through the Chapel
G School, Band room &c
H Stable
I Coach-house and Yard

was to become the mother church of Methodism. Wesley, who claimed the world as his parish, thought the building 'perfectly neat, but not fine, and [it] contains far more people than the Foundery'. Barred from preaching in churches, Wesley addressed the crowds in churchyards and fields throughout the country. In 1739 he had leased a derelict foundry nearby, which he described as 'a vast uncouth heap of ruins', to seat his rapidly growing followers. Some of its benches are still used in the side Foundry chapel to this day. Inside the new chapel, Wesley preached from a magnificent three-decker mahogany pulpit to a congregation in which men and women sat separately, and sang their hymns unaccompanied, guided by a tuning fork. The fine interior is basically still eighteenth-century though the gilded Adam ceiling is a replica of the original, which was damaged by fire. Along the base of the gallery runs a frieze with a motif of a dove symbolizing peace encircled by the serpent of healing. The gallery pillars are now of French jasper given by Methodist churches abroad, while the ships' masts they replaced (donated by George III) are part of the vestibule inserted in 1891. In that year a bronze statue of Wesley, by John Adams Acton, was erected in the forecourt to commemorate the centenary of his death.

WESLEY'S HOUSE

At 47 City Road, an eighteenth-century house now a museum, Wesley spent the winter months of his last years. Here can be seen his study, with the walnut mirrored bureau he worked at, and his bedroom. He used to rise at four in the morning to pray in this tiny chamber, with its Queen Anne table and candlestick, set in front of a window which then looked out on open fields. In the collection of Wesleyana there is a teapot specially made for Wesley by Josiah Wedgwood.

Behind the chapel lies a graveyard where Wesley was buried early one morning by torch- and lantern-light. Nearby, the supporters of George Whitefield – one of Wesley's early followers – had built him a large tabernacle in Moorfields after he left the Methodists in 1741. Whitefield later became chaplain to the Countess of Huntingdon, who built and endowed many chapels for him.

BUNHILL FIELDS

On the gateposts facing City Road are recorded the names of some of the many dissenters who were buried in Bunhill Fields between 1665 and 1852. In this former burial ground lie descendants of

Cromwell, puritans such as Thankful Owen, and the beautiful
Quakeress Hestor Savory, whom Charles Lamb so admired and
wrote about:

> *When maidens such as Hester die*
> *Their place ye may not well supply,*
> *Though ye among a thousand try*
> *With vain endeavour.*

The herald-like tombstones are marshalled row upon row –
some square-headed, others round-headed – more often than not
leaning in some direction. In the central clearing of this cemetery,
remarkable for its lack of luxurious adornment, three tombstones
stand in prime position. One is that of William Blake, the poet;
his wife is said to be about twenty yards away from the spot where
he was buried. Side panels of Christian in *Pilgrim's Progress*
indicate John Bunyan's vault; and in 1870 a marble obelisk was
placed on Daniel Defoe's tomb – 139 years after he died. Susannah
Wesley, mother of Charles and John, is buried under the trees to
the south. To the west, now surrounded by tall blocks of council
housing in Banner and Roscoe Streets, is the Quaker burial
ground where George Fox, in a plain wooden box with no bier
or cover, was given a simple funeral in 1690. In 1881 the cemetery
was laid out as a garden and a small stone marks the traditional
spot of Fox's grave.

ST LUKE'S PARISH CHURCH

The parish church of St Luke's, the pride of the surrounding
neighbourhood in the eighteenth century, now stands forlorn
with neither roof nor parish! It lost both these in 1959 when the
church was dismantled, owing to subsidence, and the parish was
amalgamated with that of St Giles Cripplegate, out of which it
had originally been carved. The fluted obelisk of this church
reaches to the sky with 'robust originality', in Pevsner's words,
but others think the steeple odd and incorrect. The church by
Hawksmoor and John James was one of fifty new churches built
between 1727 and 1733 to commemorate the campaigns of the
Duke of Marlborough; Arthur Pinero drew on the memorial
inscriptions for the names of his characters in *Trelawny of the
Wells*.

ST LUKE'S HOSPITAL

To the east of the church was St Luke's Hospital in Old Street, with its classical front in yellow brick designed by George Dance the younger. The building served as a lunatic asylum from 1787 to 1916 when the Bank of England took it over to print notes; in 1963 the Bank's printing works (which had still kept the fine facade) was demolished to make way for part of St Luke's housing estate.

PEERLESS POOL

Immediately behind St Luke's Hospital was a pond supplied by a spring, which as early as 1598 was known as the Perillous Pond since several boys had been drowned there. William Kemp, a jeweller, had the commercial sense to rename the dangerous pond the 'Peerless' pool (now a street name), and opened it in 1743 as a swimming bath nearly sixty yards long and more than thirty yards wide. He claimed his pool was the 'largest in England' within ten minutes' direct walk of the Bank and the Exchange. In 1826 William Hone, author of *Every-day Book*, described the baths as still being the same size and with enough trees to shade bathers from the heat of the sun. 'On a summer evening,' he related, 'it is amusing to survey the conduct of the bathers; some boldly dive, others "timorous stand", and then descend step by step, "unwilling and slow"; choice swimmers attract attention by divings and somersets, and the whole sheet of water sometimes rings with merriment. Every fine Thursday and Saturday afternoon in the summer, columns of blue-coat boys, more than three score in each, headed by their respective beadles, arrive, and some half strip ere they reach their destination; the rapid plunges they make into the Pool and their hilarity in the bath, testify their enjoyment of the tepid fluid.' About 1860 the pool and its adjoining fish-pond were built over.

CITY ROAD

Moorfields Eye Hospital, founded in Charterhouse Square in 1805, moved to the City Road in 1899; and a few years later, in 1904, the Leysian Mission also moved there. David Copperfield had lodged in 'Windsor Terrace' in the City Road with the Micawbers, whose servant girl came from the nearby St Luke's workhouse. Thomas Rouse built the Eagle in 1825 on the site of the 'Shepherd and Shepherdess' tea-gardens, between the City Road and Shepherdess Walk; this tavern with its Grecian saloon was eventually to become a Salvation Army citadel. It was here that this nursery rhyme originated:

> *Half a pound of tuppenny rice,*
> *Half a pound of treacle,*
> *That's the way the money goes,*
> *Pop goes the weasel.*
>
> *Up and down the City Road,*
> *In and out the Eagle,*
> *That's the way the money goes,*
> *Pop goes the Weasel.*

The tailors in the City Road would pawn (pop) their irons (weasels) to buy drinks in the Eagle!

CHARTERHOUSE

One of the finest examples of Tudor mansions – restored after the Second World War – still exists in Charterhouse Square, and may be seen by arrangement with the Registrar of Charterhouse. Leaded dormer windows peep over the main wall; clusters of chimney-tops give way to a squat tower, capped with a wooden cupola. Rebuilt on the site of the fourteenth-century monastery, this was the home of Sir Edward North, who collected the revenues from the monasteries Henry VIII suppressed. Later Sir Edward North's mansion became known as Howard House, when Thomas Howard, fourth Duke of Norfolk, lived here in splendour and plotted to overthrow his Queen. Through the ragstone archway, Elizabeth passed with her retinue to spend five nights as North's guest before her coronation; later she visited Norfolk – and his son, 'her good Thomas', after his father lost his head. Built on the outskirts of the City, the Charterhouse complex, as Pevsner states, still 'conveys a vivid impression of a large sixteenth-century mansion as they must have existed all round London'.

Post war Restoration

Blitzed during the Second World War, the Charterhouse is now restored to its former grandeur by Lord Mottistone and Paul Paget, without the Victorian stucco and misguided additions of post-Tudor days. The stone figures on the gables on the south front were carved by Michael Groser: in the middle, the Cross flanked by the Blessed Virgin and St Elisabeth symbolizes the medieval monastery; to the east the lion of England with figures of Elizabeth I and James I indicates the Tudor associations; and on the west Charterhouse School is represented by the badge of Thomas Sutton, its founder, and by figures of a gownboy and brother.

Carthusian Monastery

Of the Carthusian monastery, founded in 1371 by Sir Walter de Manny – a gentle, perfect knight such as Chaucer would have loved – little remains. The uncovered doorway of a monk's cell, that with the letter B, is still there; so is the chapel tower (formerly the monks' treasury), the arched outer gateway and part of the south outer boundary wall. The line of the Great Cloister may be imagined round the green of the adjoining St Bartholomew's Medical College. The lay brothers' quarters were in the Wash-house Court to the east.

De Manny's Grave

One of the exciting postwar discoveries was the position of Sir Walter de Manny's grave which had been lost for centuries; this determined the position of the monks' church. De Manny's grave, at the foot of the step in front of the altar, was traced by Lord Mottistone when he came upon a medieval squint in the monks' treasury at first-floor level in the chapter house. This squint, he reasoned, would look directly on to the altar so that the custodian of the treasury could take part in the mass. And so it did. An inscribed slab which marks his grave in the grass of Chapel Court can now be seen from the squint.

Founding of the Monastery

Sir Walter de Manny gave two pieces of land for the founding of the Charterhouse monastery a year before he died. He bought them both from St Bartholomew's Hospital: the Pardon church-yard, where the victims of the Black Death had been buried, and the adjoining Spittle Croft, also a burial ground. De Manny, born in Hainault, had followed Philippa of Hainault to England when she became Edward III's Queen, and he fought for Edward against the Scots, Flemings and French. Of his courage and chivalry there can be little doubt. Froissart, who was one of Queen Philippa's 'household clerks', tells in his Chronicles how de Manny served as Edward III's intermediary when Calais surrendered after a year's siege in 1347. In response to the King's demands, six burghers of Calais gave themselves up to save the rest of the starving citizens. These six burghers – long-established and wealthy merchants of the town – came to the King with their heads and feet bare, halters round their necks, and the keys of the town and castle in their hands. When Edward ordered their heads to be struck off immediately, de Manny pleaded for mercy and advised the King to curb his anger. He told him, 'You have a reputation for royal clemency. Do not perform an act which might tarnish it and allow you to be spoken of dishonourably.' Queen Philippa, pregnant at the time, then interceded, and in tears, pleaded, 'My dear lord, since I crossed the sea at great danger to myself, you know that I have never asked a single favour from you.' The King relented and handed the men to Philippa to do with as she pleased; after she had given them new clothes and an 'ample' dinner, she allowed them to return home.

De Manny founded the monastery at the suggestion of Michael Northburgh, Bishop of London. It had a prior and twenty-four monks who lived under a rule of silence and contemplation in their individual cells or houses. The monks, in their white habits, with a leathern girdle and great cowl, would meet for matins, mass and evensong, and for one common meal and walk on Sundays. They had to sing office very slowly in order to try the patience of their souls. As Dom Lawrence Hendriks, a Carthusian monk, commented: 'The fatigue of this nocturnal service is considerable, and the slower the singing proceeds, the greater the tax upon both physical and mental power. At London the chanting, at least in the sixteenth century, was very slow.'

Among those attracted by the strict discipline was Sir Thomas More who spent four years at Charterhouse 'in devotion and prayer' after studying at Oxford and Lincoln's Inn. There he lived 'religiously, but without vow' and learned to wear the hair shirt he kept until his death. He became Henry VIII's Lord Chancellor but was executed for refusing to recognize the King as head of the church.

Dissolution of the Monasteries

When Henry VIII dissolved the monasteries he found Prior John Houghton less co-operative than the Prior of St John's. The Carthusian monks had reluctantly sworn assent to the Act of Succession though they had opposed the divorce of Catherine of Aragon. When they were called upon to recognize the King as head of the church, they took leave of each other and dispersed, to their inevitable fate. That of the Prior was the most barbaric in execution: after being condemned to death, he was dragged from the Tower of London to Tyburn where he was hanged and disembowelled while still alive; and one of his limbs was hung over the monastery gate. He became Finsbury's first saint in 1970 when the Pope canonized the forty English martyrs.

Tudor Mansion

After Henry VIII had stripped the Charterhouse of timber, stone and glass, and fruit trees for his garden at Chelsea, Sir Edward North pulled down the monks' church to build the great hall of his courtyard mansion. John Dudley, Duke of Northumberland and father-in-law of Lady Jane Grey, owned the house briefly; then in 1565 Thomas Howard, fourth Duke of Norfolk, bought the Charterhouse and turned the mansion into Howard House by adding the Great Chamber (or Tapestry Room) and remodelling the Brothers' Library. The heraldry and motto of the Howards can still be seen in the richly gilded ceiling of the Great Chamber, restored after bomb damage. In this room, hung with Flemish tapestries, Norfolk entertained Elizabeth I; and his son entertained James I whose mother, Mary Queen of Scots, his father had hoped to marry. In 1570 Norfolk was sent to the Tower as a result of this ambition, but he was allowed to return for a year to Howard House where he promptly built a covered brick walk to his tennis court and added a screen to the Great Hall. He met

Charterhouse in Tudor times

De la Motte, the French ambassador, in the dilapidated chapel; and Ridolfi, the agent of Philip of Spain, came to Howard House by 'the Back Syde by the Long Workhouse at the furder end of the Lavendry Coort (Wash-house Court) and so up a new Payer of Stayers that goeth up to the old wardrobe and so through the Chamber where by Lady Estrange used to dine and sup'. A small figure of Ridolfi can be seen in a niche over the alley in the Wash-house Court he passed through. Norfolk, who had been under surveillance, was suddenly arrested – traditionally on the great staircase – and taken to the Tower by a 'fotecloth nag' which was waiting at the gate. He was executed in 1572.

Charterhouse School

Thomas Sutton, who had made an enormous fortune from mining and shipping coal, paid Thomas Howard, newly created Earl of Suffolk, £13,000 for the Charterhouse. He founded the 'Hospital of King James in the Charterhouse' for eighty pensioners and forty boys shortly before his death in 1611 at the age of eighty. He was buried in the north aisle of the chapel formed out of the monks' chapter house; here, in alabaster and black marble, his magnificent tomb, carved by Janssen and Stone, shows the pensioners assembled in the chapel. William Thackeray, who

Thomas Sutton

no doubt had studied it closely while a schoolboy at Charterhouse, described the monument and full-length effigy of Sutton in *The Newcomes*: 'Its grotesque carvings, monsters, heraldries, darkles and shines with the most wonderful shadows and lights. There he lies, Fundator Noster, in his ruff and gown, awaiting the great Examination Day.' Francis Carter, who had worked for Inigo Jones and was to become chief clerk of the King's works, modified Howard House for the governors of Charterhouse. They first met in 1613 and decided that the pensioners should be old servants of the King, 'decrepit or old Captaynes either at Sea or Land, Souldiers maymed or ympotent, decayed Marchaunts, men fallen into decaye through Shipwreckem Casualtie or Fyer or such evill Accident; those that have been Captives under the Turkes'. By 1629 they were compelled to define them further as being 'gentlemen by birth'; and to this day some thirty pensioners live at Charterhouse. The school moved to Godalming in 1872; among its illustrious old boys were John Wesley, the founder of Methodism, Sir William Blackstone, the jurist; and Sir Henry Havelock, of the Indian Mutiny. The Merchant Taylors school took over the buildings until 1933 when it moved to Northwood; the former headmaster's house, built in 1894 in ornate Franco-Flemish style, is now part of the Medical College of St Bartholomew the Great.

II

Finsbury: Clerkenwell and Environs

CLERKENWELL (which lies to the south-west of Islington) takes its name from the Clerks' Well, which is the only well still to be seen of the many that Stow described in this area. Fitzstephen, the English chronicler of the twelfth century, refers to the 'Clarkes' Well as one of the 'special wells in the suburbs' in 1174 when it stood against the wall of the Benedictine nunnery. The nunnery and the Priory of St John of Jerusalem had both been founded on land given in about 1140 by Jordan de Briset and his wife Muriel. These religious foundations were probably attracted by the many wells and proximity to the City: Fitzstephen said there were on the north side of London 'fields for pasture, and a delightful plain of meadow land, interspersed with flowing streams, on which stand mills, whose clack is very pleasing to the ear'. A dispute between the nuns and knights about some ten acres was resolved by Jordan de Briset with a formal settlement. In 1269 the Lord Prior seems to have made further amends by giving the nuns a water pot said to have been used at the marriage feast at Cana, where Jesus changed water into wine! In 1570 the last Prioress of the nunnery, Isabella Sackville, was buried near the high altar of the nuns' church which had become the parish church of St James before the dissolution.

Clerkenwell, with its village green and fine houses, grew from a hamlet until by the eighteenth century many town houses for City merchants made the area fashionable. To the north of Clerkenwell were tea-gardens, popular in the eighteenth century for their entertainment and the taste of countryside they offered city-dwellers. The most well-known – Sadler's Wells, with its long theatrical tradition – was situated near the wells Mr Sadler's workmen had rediscovered in 1684. Like others, such as Skinners' Well (now lost), these had been popular with parish clerks who performed their mystery plays near them in the fourteenth century. In 1390 the skinners of London performed mystery plays for three days for Richard II and his Queen. The other wells visisted by scholars and youths at that time – such as Fags' Well, Loder's Well and Rad Well – have also disappeared.

Craftsmen and traders wishing to escape the dues and regulations of the City guilds came to Finsbury – just outside the City gates. Distillers were attracted by the abundance of natural water; Gordons, in Goswell Road, and Booths, in Britton Street, still have distilleries in the district where the families first established their firms. By 1858 Clerkenwell was described as a 'second edition of Birmingham, in as much as its leading branches of business are purely of metallic character'. Here 'tinplate, barometers,

The earliest known map of London, showing Clerkenwell village

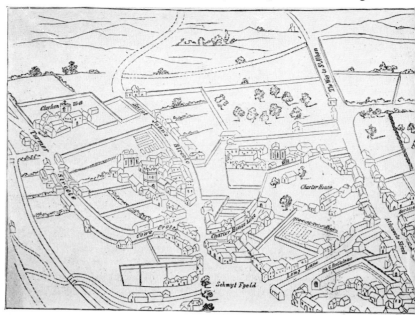

thermometers, engraving and light-printing machinery' were all part of Victorian urbanization. In the 1880s, Charles Booth documented the great poverty of those trapped in Finsbury. The Reverend William Dawson wrote in 1885: 'I have seen in upper rooms, black with the dirt of years, pale men and women sitting at bare deal boards, in front of close shut windows – the boards glittering with rubies and sapphires and emeralds, such as those of George Eliot's Dorothea thought of often having by her, "to feed her eyes with those fountains of pure colour", but over which, you will remember, that fair and gracious creature of the mighty artist's mind sighed to think of the "miserable men" who worked at them.'

To the north the Lloyd Baker and Metropolitan Board estates were laid out in the early nineteenth century. By 1891 an avenue to be called after Lord Rosebery, the first chairman of the London County Council, had been cut through the maze of streets, and Exmouth Street, no longer a main thoroughfare, became a street market. From the newly built town hall the local council administered the smallest-but-one of the London boroughs. In the 1920s the Metropolitan Water Board took over the New River which had been built by Sir Hugh Myddelton in the seventeenth century to bring water to the City of London. After the Second World War water from Amwell no longer flowed to the New River Head, now the headquarters of the Board.

CHARACTER

Some of the narrow streets of Tudor times remain though the buildings are predominantly Victorian; some neo-Gothic warehouses in St John's Lane are fine examples. The historic buildings of St John's Gate and the parish church of St James are rare examples of what Clerkenwell once was. The twentieth-century buildings of Sadler's Wells Theatre, the New Metropolitan Water Board headquarters, and the high-rise council housing schemes make this part of Islington seem more a part of modern London. Clerkenwell still has a certain village character because of its 'green', though now urbanized through the influx of industries and commerce; the area is vastly depopulated, but in some parts there are council tenants and residents.

THE CLERKS' WELL

Until 1924, when a workman found the Clerks' Well in the cellar of a warehouse in Farringdon Road, its whereabouts had been a mystery for some time! Now, on application to the Librarian at Finsbury Library, this well, so 'greatly esteemed by the prior and brethren of the order of St John of Jerusalem, and the Benedictine nuns in the neighbourhood', is open to visitors – a small blue plaque denotes its entrance. The water in the well is more or less at constant level and yet it is clear which seems to indicate that a spring still supplies it with that 'excellently clear, sweet and well tasted' water the historian Strype enjoyed in 1720. The well took its name from the clerks who performed their plays in the natural amphitheatre of the valley of the Fleet. In Stow's time it was 'curbed about square with hard stone'. In 1800 the water ran through the spout of a pump in the wall – and the iron tablet which the churchwardens placed above this pump is now in the cellar.

ST JOHN OF JERUSALEM

The grey Kentish ragstone gatehouse, which straddles St John's Lane, was the south entrance of the Priory of St John of Jerusalem. Through this gateway, rebuilt in 1504 by Prior Thomas Docwra, lies the former courtyard of the priory – now St John's Square, bisected by Clerkenwell Road in 1877. In the north-east corner of the square is St John's church; only the crypt of the original twelfth-century church remains intact. The present plain square church was reconstructed from the former choir walls, replacing an eighteenth-century parish church blitzed in 1941. The building now serves as the church and investiture hall of the Order of St John of Jerusalem, known for its work through the St John's Ambulance Association. To the south, on the site of the chapel Docwra built, is a cloister-like Garden of Remembrance; here is one of the nineteen guns Henry VIII gave to Grand Master Villiers de L'Isle Adam to launch a counter-attack on the Turks who had expelled the Order from Rhodes in 1522.

Consecration of the Church

The original church was consecrated by Heraclius, Patriarch of

Sir Thomas Docwra, builder of St John's Gate

Jerusalem in 1185. Cobblestones in the square west of the present church show where its round nave stood. Heraclius had travelled from Jerusalem to get Henry II's help for a crusade, but he failed. He then burst out to the King: 'Here is my head, treat me, if you like, as you did my brother Thomas [meaning Thomas à Becket]; it is a matter of indifference to me whether I die by your orders or in Syria by the hands of the infidels, for you are worse than a Saracen.' Henry, however, took no notice of his insolence.

Wat Tyler's Rebellion

By 1381 the Knights of the Order, once so poor that their governor was called Servant to the Poor Servants of the Hospital, had become exceedingly powerful. Richard Newcourt, author of *Repertorium Ecclesiasticum* published in 1710, relates that 'they flourished in great Pomp for many years' and 'their condition came to be so much altered ... by the Bounty of good Princes and Private Persons, that they abounded in every thing; their Prior was reckon'd the first Baron of England'. They were so hated that in 1381, after rampaging through the Fleet prison, the Temple and the Savoy, Wat Tyler and his furious mob turned their vengeance on the priory which they let burn for seven days, stopping any attempts to quench the fire. Sir Robert Hales, Prior at the time and Treasurer of England, had fled to the Tower of London where the rioters found 'Hobbe the Robber', as they nicknamed him, with the Archbishop of Canterbury and others. These they dragged out on to Tower Hill and beheaded. Richard II met the peasants at Smithfield, and riding among them promised to be their leader. Meanwhile Wat Tyler was being wounded by William Walworth, mayor of London, and Walworth later had the rebel leader dragged out from St Bartholomew's hospital and beheaded; he himself was knighted for his deed.

Restoration of the Priory

Many decades later, Thomas Docwra, Prior from 1501 to 1527, was to complete the restoration of the ransacked priory. The priory, in William Camden's words, 'resembled a palace, and had in it a very faire church and a towre steeple, raised to a great height, with so fine workmanship that it was a singular beauty

Præfata Domus a retro ab Euro-aquilone prospectus

Hollar's engraving of the Priory of St John

and ornament to the city'. Stow considered the great tower (which stood north of a rectangular nave) one of the marvels of London. The perpendicular windows, still part of the present church, were inserted by Docwra; and the gatehouse (with his coat of arms on both sides) stands as a monument to this prior who was more than once employed by Henry VIII on embassies and commissions.

His successor was less fortunate. The Knights had chosen Sir William Weston, who had fought in the siege of Rhodes, as their prior in defiance of the King. With the dissolution, Henry VIII usurped 'all the landes that belonged to that house and that Order, wheresoever in England and Ireland, for the augmentation of his crowne'. Weston did not defy the royal power as Prior John Houghton of Charterhouse had done; he was content to accept a pension, but ironically he was not to need it long. As John Weever relates: 'It fortuned on the 7th day of May, 1540, being Ascension Day, and the same day as the dissolution of his house, he was dissolved by death, which strooke him to the heart at the first time when he heard of the dissolution of his Order.' Weston was buried in St James's church nearby; his emaciated form lies in an effigy on his tomb now in the crypt of St John's church.

The Priory as Store House and Royal Palace

Henry VIII turned the priory into a store house for his hunting tents and nets. The church and tower were later demolished with gunpowder by the Duke of Somerset, Protector to Edward VI, who used the stone to build a palace in the Strand: Somerset House. But he was not to live to see its completion since he was executed earlier. As Sir Henry Spelman commented: '. . . the curse of sacrilege cleaves to consecrated stone . . . so as the builder does not finish his house nor doth his son inherit it'. Princess Mary seems to have lived at the priory after her father's death; she is shown setting out to see her brother Edward VI in a tiled scene in the Metropolitan Tavern (at the corner of Farringdon Road and Clerkenwell Road). Henry Machyn, a merchant tailor, recorded in 1551: 'The XV the day the Lady Mary rode through London into St John's, her place, with fifty knights and gentlemen and ladies, every one having a peyre of beads of black.'

Soon after she became Queen, Mary, as a devout Catholic, not only revived the Order of St John, but saw that the church plundered by Somerset was repaired, the building being fore-shortened with a new west front. Here in 1555 – with 'the quyre honge with cloth of arres' – mass was once more celebrated. When Elizabeth succeeded her sister, she was quick to confiscate the estates from the Knights Hospitallers and she turned the priory into an office for her Master of Revels, Edmund Tylney. Here he licensed plays and was probably visited by Ben Jonson, Marlowe and Shakespeare; in the great hall he rehearsed the entertainments for the Court.

The Gentleman's Magazine

From 1733 until 1781 the *Gentleman's Magazine*, with a print of St John's Gate on its cover, was published here; David Garrick, the actor, gave his first dramatic performance in London to the workmen of Edward Cave, the owner and editor; and Samuel Johnson, who had taught him Latin and Greek, wrote Parlia-mentary sketches with the Members' names in anagram form to evade the law. William Hogarth's father kept a coffee house in St John's Gate for a brief time early in the eighteenth century and was 'always ready to entertain Gentlemen in the Latin Tongue'. Hogarth spent part of his childhood in Clerkenwell; and as he recorded in his autobiography: 'An early access to a neighbouring painter drew my attention from play; and I was, at every possible opportunity, employed in making drawings.' His friend John Wilkes, whom he later savagely caricatured, was born in 1727 to the north in St John's Square where his father was a distiller. Dr Gilbert Burnet, former Bishop of Salisbury and a staunch upholder of the Reformation, lived his last years in St John's Square; there he saw the contents of the chapel, then used as a Presbyterian meeting-house, dragged out and burnt before the door by the Sacheverell rioters in 1710.

Order of St John of Jerusalem

Since 1873 when it was reconstituted, the gatehouse has been the headquarters of the Order of St John of Jerusalem. In the re-panelled Council Chamber over St John's Lane are recorded the

The Gentleman's Magazine:

St John's Gate.

London Gazette
Londō Jour.
Fog's Journ.
Applebee's ::
Read's ::::
Craftsman ::
D. Spectator
Senbstreet J.
W.ly Register
Free-Briton.
Uni- Doctor
Daily Courāt
Daily Post.:
Dat. Journal
Dat. Post-boy
D. Advertiser
Evening Post
St James's Eb.
Whitehall Eb.
Lōdon Ebēsq
Flying-Post

York Journals
Dublin ditto
Edinburgh 2
Norwich two
Exeter two:
Worcester 2.:
Northamptō
Gloucester ::
Stamford::
Nottingham
Bristol News
Bury Journ.
Ipswich do.
Chester ditto
Leeds Merc.
Newcastle C.
Derby Journ.
Reading ditto
Canterbury
Boston ::: b
Jamaica, &c.

Or, Monthly Intelligencer.

Number I. for JANUARY, 1731.

CONTAINING,

more in Quantity, and greater Variety, than any Book of the Kind and Price.

I. A View of the Weekly *Essays* and *Controversies*, viz. Of Q. *Elizabeth*; Ministers; Treaties; Liberty of the Press; Riot Act; Armies; Traytors; Patriots; Reason; Criticism; Versifying; Ridicule; Humours; Love; Prostitutes; Music; Pawn-brokers; Surgery; Law.

II. POETRY, *viz.* The *Ode* for the New Year, by *Colly Cibber*, Esq; Remarks upon it; Imitations of it, by way of *Burlesque*; Verses on the same Subject; ingenious Epitaphs and Epigrams.

III. *Domestick* Occurrences, *viz.* Births, Deaths, Marriages, Preferments, Casualties, Burials and Christenings in *London.*

IV. Melancholy Effects of Credulity in *Witchcraft.*

V. Prices of Goods and Stocks, and a List of Bankrupts.

VI. A correct List of the Sheriffs for the current Year.

VII. Remarkable *Advertisements.*

VIII. *Foreign* Affairs, with an Introduction to this Year's History.

IX. Books and Pamphlets publish'd.

X. Observations on *Gardening*, and a List of Fairs for the Season.

With a *Table* of *Contents.*

By SYLVANUS URBAN, Gent.

The Fourth Edition.

LONDON, Printed and Sold at *St John's Gate*, by F. *Jefferies* in *Ludgate-street*; and most Booksellers in Town and Country. 1732. (Price 6 d.)

Note, *A few are printed on fine Royal Paper, large Margin, for the Curious.*

names of eminent members such as Florence Nightingale, Lady
Mountbatten and Sir John Furley, who was responsible for the
first stretcher. On the east side is a Tudor-style building of 1903
by John Oldrid Scott where the panelling in the chapter hall is
embellished with the arms of all the priors from Prior Walter
to the Duke of Gloucester.

Cock Lane Ghost

The gatehouse, which also has a library and museum, and the
church, may be seen by appointment. The twelfth-century crypt
of the church is now a memorial chapel of St John Almoner (the
original patron saint of the Order). Here in 1763 Samuel Johnson
was disappointed in his attempt to hear the ghost of 'Scratching
Fanny' said to be buried with Frances Lynes. This ghost was
first heard in Cock Lane where Frances Lynes had lived with her
lover, who was also a brother-in-law; crowds flocked to hear the
ghost interpreted by the landlord's daughter after Frances Lynes's
death. 'I went to hear it,' Horace Walpole wrote to Montague in
1781, 'for it is not an apparation, but an audition. We set out from
the opera, changed our clothes at Northumberland House. The
Duke of York, Lady Northumberland, Lady Mary Coke, Lady
Hertford and I, all in a hackney-coach, drove to the spot. It
rained in torrents; yet the lane was full of mob, and the houses
full. We could not get in. At last they discovered it was the Duke
of York; and the company squeezed themselves into one another's
pockets to make room for us. The house which is borrowed, and
to which the ghost had adjourned, is wretchedly small and miserable. When we opened the chamber, in which were fifty people,
with no light but one tallow-candle at the end, we tumbled over
the bed of the child to whom the ghost comes. At the top of the
room are ropes to dry clothes. I asked if we were to have rope-
dancing between the acts. We heard nothing. We staid till half-
an-hour after one. Provisions are sent in like forage, and all the
taverns and alehouses in the neighbourhood make fortunes.'
The church has two panels of a fine triptych of the Roger
van der Weyden School; these panels of fifteenth-century
Flemish art were given to the church in 1480 by Grand Prior
John Weston to commemorate the Order's victory at Rhodes
that year.

CLERKENWELL GREEN

Though there is no longer a pillory or watch-house on Clerkenwell Green, the odd-shaped houses huddling round the traffic islands with a horse water-trough and a gas-lamp standard offer a glimpse of the village centre this once was. To the north, Clerkenwell Close, formerly a path with turnstile, leads to the parish church; on the same side the classical-fronted No. 37a was a charity school for a time; and to the west the court-house used until 1920 still stands. William Pinks records that in the seventeenth century the green was 'environed by the mansions of the noble and affluent, who sought and found a comparative seclusion from society in the rural suburb of Clerkenwell; the footpaths in front of the houses were skirted by lofty trees, many of which still flourished at a period within memory'.

In 1650 and 1651 Izaak Walton had two sons baptised at the parish church but both – called Izaak – died within the year; in 1653, Walton, a linen-draper who had retired to Clerkenwell with his second wife, published the fisherman's classic, *The Compleat Angler*.

Among the many from the City who made the Green a fashionable address at that time was Sir Richard Cheverton, who, as Lord Mayor of London, had proclaimed Cromwell's son, Richard, Protector in 1658. After the Great Fire of London, Clerkenwell – then a village of 416 houses – nearly trebled itself in fifty years.

Political Meetings

By the early nineteenth century Clerkenwell Green had become a mini Hyde Park Corner where the early trade unionists and radicals delivered their soap-box oratory. John Wilkes, who represented Middlesex (which included Finsbury at that time), spoke at the Green against his expulsion from the Commons in 1764; and here in 1826 William Cobbett, the champion of Radicalism, criticized the Corn Laws. In 1832 the crowds cheered Lovett, Watson and Benbow, leaders of the National Union of the Working Class, after their acquittal at the Sessions House of a charge of creating 'with force and arms . . . a great riot, tumult and disturbance'. In 1833 when a coroner's jury found 'the conduct of the police . . . ferocious, brutal and unprovoked by the

FINSBURY ELECTION: THE NOMINATION ON CLERKENWELL GREEN.

people' after a policeman had been killed in an attempt to break up a demonstration elsewhere in Clerkenwell, the crowd roared their endorsement of the verdict. Peel prevented the Chartists from speaking at Clerkenwell Green in 1842; and three Chartist workmen who had made seditious speeches there were sentenced in 1848 to two years' imprisonment. During the summer that year there were many struggles with the police, and one night the Horse Guards occupied the Green. James Cornish, a policeman at the time, later recalled that 'there was plenty of open space on the Green for fighting, and many houses in which Chartists could hide and throw things at us'. In 1866 and 1867 thousands met at Clerkenwell Green before going to Hyde Park to demonstrate their support for the Reform League in its fight for a better franchise.

London Patriotic Club

No wonder then that one of the first Radical working men's clubs – the London Patriotic Club – met at 37a Clerkenwell Green! Among its backers was John Stuart Mill, the philosopher and radical reformer, who had learnt Greek at the age of three from his father in Rodney Street, Pentonville. In 1872, a year before his death, he gave £20 to the Club to find 'a place for political lectures and discussions, independent of tavern-keepers and licensing magistrates'. When the Twentieth Century Press, the socialist publishers, took over the building from 1893 to 1922, William Morris, the craftsman and poet, acted as a guarantor for the first year's rent.

Associations with Lenin

To this building Lenin – then known as Vladimir Ilyich Ulyanov – came to correct the proofs of the revolutionary newspaper, *Iskra*, during 1902 and 1903. Lenin, who had been in exile in Switzerland, lived in Holford Square with his wife Krupskaya while he was in London; he would sit at a very small writing-table in a corner boarded off from the printing-works, while he read through the newspaper which had been set by a Russian compositor in the East End. In 1905, after becoming leader of the Bolsheviks, he returned briefly to London for the third conference of the Russian Social Democratic Party and stayed in Percy Circus where a blue plaque records the event. The Marx Memorial Library opened with about 5,000 books on socialism in 1933 in this building, and in its first years arranged that Karl Marx's death should be commemorated every year at Highgate cemetery where he is buried. In 1969 the façade was restored so that James Steere's design for the Welsh charity school, which originally used the building, is plain. This school was founded by the Honourable and Loyal Society of Antient Britons under the Prince of Wales's patronage to teach the three R's to poor Welsh children before apprenticing them; the school, which was here from 1737 to 1772, is now the Welsh Girls' School at Ashford, Middlesex.

Sessions House

On the west side of the green is the former Sessions House, which

The Sessions House

replaced Hicks Hall, built in St John's Lane by Sir Baptist Hicks for the magistrates of James I's reign. Though the Palladian front is an imposing one, the building loses some of its majestic appeal by being situated on a slope rather than a hill. As the sculptural reliefs by Nollekens indicate, justice and mercy were dispensed here from 1782 when George III was King. The magistrates in Victorian times appear to have needed more room to deal with cases since the building was altered and enlarged in 1860 by F. H. Pownall. They sat here until 1920 when they moved to Newington Causeway, south of the river. The design for the front is by John Carter, who drew for the *Builder's Magazine*. He published drawings for a sessions house in one of its issues which Thomas Rogers copied and sent in as his own for a competition for the new Sessions House. This cribbed design won the competition while, ironically, another drawing which Carter had submitted as his own entry was rejected!

Watch-Making Industry

Clerkenwell Green is a small shop-window for the watch-making industry which formerly flourished in the district. On the south side antique clocks have pride of place in a shop-front. In the Crown, on the north side, the landlord has a collection of ships' clocks, grandfather clocks and railway clocks peering solemnly down, showing the time in such exotic cities as Peking, Rangoon and Baghdad. At one time a Clerkenwell face was so sought after that French and German clocks were sent to London to be finished off. Skilled craftsmen specialized in making the many delicate parts such as jewels, pinions and wheels which in due course were to make up the prized possessions of the rich. Christopher Pinchbeck, the clockmaker, who lived in St George's Court (now Albion Place) in 1721, invented the alloy of copper and zinc named after him. Messrs Thwaites and Reed, one of the few firms still left, were established in Bowling Green Lane in 1740 and now service such clocks as Big Ben and Bow Bell.

ST JAMES'S PARISH CHURCH

The parish church of Clerkenwell, with its stone steeple still visible above the roof tops, is the north of Clerkenwell Green in the twisting Clerkenwell Close. On its site stood the church where the Benedictine nuns, in their black robes and cowls, worshipped. Much of the Dutch-like character of this narrow close has gone, with only a few terraced houses remaining – the rest, including some weavers' cottages with wide attic windows to catch the most light, have disappeared. The present church is a plain stock-brick box designed in 1792 by James Carr, one of the most respected Palladian architects of the period. The steeple, which Basil Clarke thinks 'rather lonely in Clerkenwell as though it had strayed from the City', was rebuilt in 1849 without altering the open octagonal stage, topped by a smaller concave one and then an obelisk spire. Inside the entrance the benefactions to poor widows, unmarried female orphans, and poor children are listed in dull gold letters on black boards for all to read: they are no longer given in the form of bread, coals and warm clothing but in money to the needy. The colourful (some think garish) east window showing the Ascension of Christ, with its emphasis, that

St James's Church, Clerkenwell

some evangelicals dislike, on the figure of Mary, dates from 1863. Otherwise the interior is classical eighteenth-century in character. Since the Smithfield Martyrs Memorial Church in St John Street has gone, the names of the martyrs burned at Smithfield are recorded here. Set in the east wall is part of the tombstone of the Countess Dowager of Exeter who died in 1653, 'an example for piety, wisdom, bounty, charity, and all goodness fit for imitation of all ladies of honour and virtue'. She was the widow of William Cecil, the grandson of William, Lord Burghley, who was Elizabeth's Lord Treasurer. As Lady Burghley she had been 'very forward to repair the ruined choir' of St John's church. William Wood, well-known for his archery textbook *The Bowmen's Glory, or Archery Revived*, was buried in the churchyard in 1691 with full archers' honours – three flights of arrows giving a loud whistling sound over his grave!

CLERKENWELL HOUSE OF DETENTION

The boundary walls of the Clerkenwell House of Detention followed much the same line as those which now surround the red-brick Victorian building of Hugh Myddelton School, with Corporation Row to the north, and Sans Walk to the south. In the south-east corner the former governor's house, with all its windows facing inwards, is built into the outer wall.

Fenian Plot

On the afternoon of Friday, 13 December 1867, three men wheeled a beer cask of explosive covered with a white cloth and placed it on the pavement beside the northern wall of the Clerkenwell House of Detention. In the failing light they managed to place a lighted squib in the barrel, and ran off down the narrow, crowded street that Corporation Row then was. The explosion which followed was devastatingly successful in blowing a vast breach in the prison wall; it wrecked the whole row of working-class tenements opposite, and killed six people immediately; eleven more died later and some 150 were injured. But in their object of rescuing the Fenian prisoners, Burke and Casey, awaiting trial for subversive activities, the conspirators failed; theirs was 'a crime of unexampled atrocity' as *The Times* commented the following day. 'Till yesterday', the paper stated in its leader, 'we could not have believed that there lived among us men capable of planning such a deed as has just spread destruction over a whole neighbourhood. The Infernal Machines of 1800 and 1835 have been rivalled by the diabolical device of the Fenian conspirators. In order, as it is supposed, to rescue two of their accomplices . . . it has entered into the minds of the rebels who are planning the overthrow of the Queen's Government in Ireland to destroy the wall of the prison at the moment the prisoners were taking exercise, and to carry them off through the gap which the explosion should create.' A few months previously the Fenians had rescued two prisoners from a prison van in Manchester; their plot at Clerkenwell was foiled by the Governor, who, following a tip-off, altered the Irish prisoners' exercise period from the afternoon to the morning, and arranged extra outside patrols. As a result, three were arrested straightaway and eventually six stood trial, among whom was Michael Barrett who emerged as the ring-leader and was the only one to be executed. Ironically, his was the last public execution in England: on 26 May 1868, with the crowd shouting 'Hats off', Michael Barrett was hanged on a scaffold above the main gate of Newgate jail.

Gordon Riots

The House of Detention (1845–77) replaced the New Prison, first built next to the Clerkenwell Bridewell (1615–1804), but towards the end of the eighteenth century this House of Detention was extended and enlarged, taking over the site of the demolished Clerkenwell Bridewell. Here, during the Gordon riots of 1780, the crowd broke into the prison and released all the prisoners.

NEWCASTLE HOUSE

Just north of the old nuns' church stood Newcastle House: 'spacious, and stately, though somewhat gloomy-looking', which the Duke of Newcastle built largely from the ruins of the nunnery. William Cavendish was made a duke after the Restoration by Charles II whom he entertained at Newcastle House in 1667; during the Civil War he and his Newcastle Lambs had fought valiantly but in vain for Charles I.

Newcastle House

His blue-stocking second wife, Margaret Lucas, had such a 'passion for scribbling' that she had a servant sleeping nearby ready to put her thoughts on paper during the night. The Duchess was the talk of the town and Pepys noted: 'The whole story of this lady is a romance, and all she does is romantic.' In his diary of 26 April 1667 he wrote: 'Met my Lady Newcastle going with her coachmen and footmen all in velvet: herself, whom I never saw before, as I have heard her often described, for all the town-talk is now-a-days of her extravagancies, with her velvet-cap, her hair about her ears, many black patches, because of pimples about her mouth; naked-necked, without any thing about it, and a black just-au-corps.' A few days later, on 1 May 1667, he wrote: 'She was in a large black coach, adorned with silver instead of gold, and so white curtains, and every thing black and white, and herself in her cap.' Pepys read her 'ridiculous history of my Lord Newcastle' which he thought 'shows her to be a mad,

William Cavendish Duke of Newcastle

conceited, ridiculous woman, and he an asse to suffer her to write what she writes to him and of him'. The Duke, once complimented on the wisdom of his wife, is said to have replied, 'Sir, a very wise woman is a very foolish thing.' His grand-daughter, Elizabeth, the 'mad' Duchess of Albemarle, died at Newcastle House. After the death of her first husband, the Duke of Albemarle, she was 'so inflated with vanity by the possession of much wealth' that she would only marry a sovereign prince. Ralph, first Duke of Montague, succeeded where other suitors failed by pretending to be the Emperor of China! After their marriage he shared her wealth, but not her affections for he kept her confined in Montague House. She survived him by some thirty years. Newcastle House was demolished about 1793 and replaced in part by handsome houses in Newcastle Place.

PRESENT CLERKENWELL

One of the most charming streets in the neighbourhood is Sekforde Street in which the Pall-Mall-like front of the former Finsbury Bank for Savings was an advertisement for thrifty passers-by to see. Near Woodbridge Street, which intersects the curving Sekforde Street, stood the Red Bull, an Elizabethan playhouse known for its comic pieces; but when Pepys visited it the audience numbered less than a hundred. Jerusalem Passage, with its Crusade associations, narrows to the south with a fine view of St John's Gate. In Cowcross Street, near Smithfield Market, is the Castle – now a modern public house – where George IV pawned his watch after losing money at a cockfight, as a painting inside shows. The King was returned his watch, and the landlord was granted a pawnbroker's licence which his successor holds to this day. Between Turnmill Street and Britton Street is the tiny St John's Gardens, formerly a graveyard belonging to St John's church, which since 1881 has been 'a garden for the quiet enjoyment and refreshment of the living, especially of the dwellers in its densely peopled neighbourhood'. To the north these gardens are overlooked by the re-erected art nouveau façade of the former Booth's gin distillery. A frieze of five bas-reliefs by F. R. Pomeroy denotes the process of gin-making from reaping corn to tapping the oak.

MAKING OF THE NEW RIVER

The red-brick neo-Georgian headquarters of the Metropolitan Water Board were built in 1920 over the site of the Round Pond's basin, part of which still hems the building like a quay. The water of the New River first flowed from Amwell into this pond, which formed the New River Head, in 1613. At the opening ceremony some sixty labourers, 'well apparelled, and wearing green Monmouth caps', carrying spades, shovels and pickaxes, marched to drums round the cistern. Hugh Myddelton, who had created the City's most important water source, was to be honoured in many ways in time to come: most important of all, his water-course still forms about an eighth of London's water supply. But during his lifetime, even though he had the King's patronage, he reaped few dividends and little glory apart from a baronetcy.

Hugh Myddelton

Myddelton had come to London from Denbighshire to make his fortune, as several of his brothers were to do. He was apprenticed to a goldsmith and became Warden in 1604, and later twice Prime Warden of the Goldsmith's Company. He dealt with the Court, supplying Queen Elizabeth with a 'carcanet of pearle' and Queen Anne, wife of James I, with a diamond pendant. Like his brothers, he became a Member of Parliament. In 1609 he found an enterprise which was to consume his energies for the rest of his life: that year he wrote: 'I have undertaken a matter, which I praye God prosper, that will cost me all my poor meanese, this berer will enforme you thereof, I cannot be Idell.' The matter was the New River.

Course of the New River

In 1604 the City had encouraged Edmond Colthurst to build a river drawing water from Hertfordshire springs since the existing sources were inadequate. Five years later Colthurst's project had not advanced much, and the City turned to Myddelton with his

The Old Water House and pond at New River Head

'Sir Hugh Myddelton's Glory', New River Head, 1613

greater financial skill to 'undertake the same worke', provided
he finished within four years. All went well for several months
until Myddelton ran into the opposition of stubborn landlords
who objected to the course running through *their* land! They
nearly succeeded in having a repealing act passed through Parliament but, fortunately for Myddelton, Parliament was dissolved
in 1611, and by the time the next Parliament met, he had finished
his New River. By 1612 he also had the support of James I as a
business partner which meant that 'tumultuous or other undue
or unlawful courses' in 'hindrance, lett or opposition' to the work
could be quickly quelled. In its thirty-eight miles from Amwell
to Clerkenwell the course was so accurately surveyed that there
was only a drop of about eighteen feet. The water ran through a
wooden aqueduct, 'the Boarded River', in Highbury. The water,
from springs at Amwell and Chadwell, and the River Lee, was
distributed from the Round Pond at Clerkenwell by means of
wooden pipes to individual houses and conduits. Though Myddelton had freed consumers from using 'foule and unwholesome

water which breedeth great infections' they preferred the water supplied by water-carriers with their cry of 'Fresh and fair new river-water. None of your pipe sludge'. James was not too pleased with this situation and in 1616 his Privy Council rapped the City authorities. Though the New River Company was granted a royal charter in 1619, James had to wait until 1622 for his first dividend. His son, Charles, sold his share in 1630 in return for a £500 annuity, known as the King's Clog, which the Metropolitan Water Board redeemed in 1956. In 1904 the Board paid some £6 million for the enterprise which had cost Myddelton some £18,500.

New River Company's Board Room

Within the headquarters, built by Austen Hall, the oak-panelled

The Oak Room at New River Head, showing the carvings attributed to Grinling Gibbons

board room of the New River Company may be seen on application to the Secretary. The richly carved black oak subjects, pheasant and lobster among them, are attributed to Grinling Gibbons. The moulded seventeenth-century ceiling (at which some members of the Board no doubt gazed!) shows subjects associated with rivers, such as fishermen and swans. In the centre is an oval portrait of William III surrounded by allegorical figures, painted by Henry Cooke, a court painter; and the arms of this King are over the mantelpiece. The room was originally part of the old Water House where the company's surveyors (or engineers) lived for a time – the most notable being Robert Mylne, the architect of Blackfriars Bridge and father of William Chadwell Mylne, who laid out the New River Company's estates to the north. Howard Robertson designed the curved research building in 1938, which overlooks a lily pond. For some years after the Claremont Square reservoir was built in 1709, a windmill pumped the water, but later a steam pump in the Engine House installed by Smeaton did the work. The last filter-bed was abandoned in 1946 when the New River stopped at Stoke Newington, though parts of its course through Islington can still be traced in the New River Walk through Canonbury.

DAME ALICE OWEN

The Tudor gateposts of the school that Dame Alice Owen founded more than three centuries ago now face Goswell Road – her first almshouses and school fronted on to St John Street. As a girl of fifteen Alice Wilkes had gone for a walk with a maidservant in the fields where the Victorian boys' school and the girls' school (rebuilt in the 1960s) now stand. No doubt she knew the fields well, as her father, Thomas Wilkes, was a tenant-occupier of land in Barnsbury and she herself had been born in Islington in 1547. On their walk they saw a woman milking a cow, and Alice thought she would have a go at milking. The place was in the middle of the Butts, and as she got up from the milking stool, an arrow shot William Tell-like through her hat, narrowly missing her head. Alice was so relieved that she vowed that if she lived to be a lady she would 'erect something on that spot of ground in commemoration of the great mercy shown by the Almighty in that astonishing deliverance'.

School and Almshouses

She fulfilled her vow shortly before her death in 1613 by building almshouses for 'ten poor widows' who were to receive an allowance of 'sea-coal' and one gown each 'of three yards of broad cloth' once in two years. The school, for which she herself drew up orders and rules, was a free grammar school for thirty boys – twenty-four from Islington and six from Clerkenwell. She was in a position to be generous as she had been widowed three times, and her first two husbands, Henry Robinson and William Elkin, both brewers, had left her well-off. She bought the eleven acres of 'Ermitage Fields' in 1608 and left the administration in the hands of the Brewers Company. Ironically, she was never to be a lady as her third husband, Thomas Owen, a judge of the Court of the Common Pleas to Queen Elizabeth, died shortly before he was to be knighted. One of her daughters, Ursula Elkin, however, married Sir Roger Owen (her step-son) and so became a lady!

Frampton Statue of Dame Alice

In the lobby of the boys' school stands a statue of Dame Alice by George Frampton, who sculpted the Peter Pan statue in Kensington Gardens. His work of Dame Alice unveiled in 1897 is an interesting example of the new English School of Sculpture which used materials other than white marble. The head of marble with its benign expression shows Dame Alice's kindness: the richness of Tudor dress pervades the bronze figure; while in her alabaster hands she carries a life-like prayer book and walking stick. Part of the inscription from her tomb in St Mary's parish church is on the base of the statue, telling of her generosity especially in Islington where stood 'a monument of her piety to future ages', 'more worthie and largelie expressing her pietie than these gowlden letters, as much as deedes are above wordes'. Between two pomegranate trees from her coat of arms, and set in the wall above the statue, are nine figures formerly on her tomb. These figures are some of the twelve children and many grand-children she had also 'advanced and enriched'. In 1886 girls were to benefit from her foundation when Dame Alice Owen's Girls' school opened in a building by E. H. Martineau in Owen's Row.

During the Second World War the building, used as an air-raid shelter, was destroyed in the Blitz with many casualties. Both schools are now in the process of moving to Potters' Bar, away from the spot where Dame Alice made her original vow. From 1786 to 1825 the Friends' School, now in Saffron Walden, was south-east of the site of Dame Alice Owen's schools in Goswell Road – and – Friend Street nearby is a reminder of this school founded in 1702 as a workhouse for the old and a school for the young in Bowling Green Lane.

ISLINGTON SPA

Of the tea-gardens round the fringe of Spa Fields, where now post war council housing fronts on to public gardens, little remains. In the eighteenth century these drew pleasure-seekers ranging from the *beau monde* to bourgeois publicans and tradesmen. In 1733 Princess Amelia, George II's daughter, spent her birthday at Islington Spa (this site is marked by a plaque in Lloyd's Row); she and her sister Caroline were so attracted to it that they went there daily during June that year and 'such was the concourse of nobility and others, that the proprietor took above £30 in one morning'! Others, such as Mrs Rubrick in George Coleman's farce *The Spleen*, or *Islington Spa* (first acted in 1776), went for the walks, balls, raffles and dinners. 'The wateringplaces', she comments, 'are the only places to get young women lovers and husbands!' Malcolm, writing in 1803, described the gardens of Islington Spa as 'really very beautiful, particularly at the entrance. Pedestals and vases are grouped with taste under some extremely picturesque trees, whose foliage [is] seen to much advantage from the neighbouring fields'. Near the site of Islington Spa (1684 to *c.* 1840), opposite Sadler's Wells, Deacon's Music Hall flourished between 1860 and 1891 when it was demolished to make way for Rosebery Avenue.

Other Tea-Gardens

As the owners competed for the custom of the city crowds, they provided entertainment ranging from bands to variety acts, and wonders such as zoos or grottos for gaping sightseers. The London Spa, on the site of the public house on the corner of

Rosoman and Exmouth Streets, was popular with May-dancers in the 1720s; later the tavern with its 'usual entertainment of roast pork with the oft-famed flavoured Spaw ale' drew scores from the Welsh fairs in Spa Fields. At the New Wells to the south of the London Spa there was 'a fine collection of large rattlesnakes, one having nineteen rattles, and seven young ones, a young crocodile imported from Georgia, American darting and flying squirrels, which may be handled as any of our own, and a cat between the tiger and leopard, perfectly tame, and one of the most beautiful creatures that ever was in England'. In the theatre there Rosoman (who later owned Sadler's Wells and built part of Rosoman Street) played Harlequin, and Madam Kerman, a tight-rope walker, danced on stilts! The English Grotto had a water grotto garden; the Mulberry Garden had avenues round a tree said to date from James I's reign; and Merlin's Cave – south of the modern public house – probably had a cave imitating the one Queen Charlotte built at Richmond in 1735.

SADLER'S WELLS

At the top of Rosebery Avenue is Sadler's Wells Theatre, now a red-bricked building, with a semi-circular relief showing Grecian maidens drawing water from a well over its entrance. Here, towards the end of the seventeenth century Mr Sadler owned a long low wooden music-house set in its own gardens north of the New River. In 1683 his workmen uncovered a 'large well of stone arched over and curiously carved'. So popular was the mineral water from this well that Sadler soon became the scourge of rival spa-owners at Epsom and Tunbridge; and Nahum Tate, dramatist and later poet laureate, scathingly referred to his wells as 'Sadler's pump'. In a pamphlet the spa-owners advised Islington to stick to its traditional trade of 'cakes, custards and stewed pruans'! But Sadler, who had advertised the pleasures of his waters – one could eat carraways while drinking it or have a glass of Rhenish or white wine afterwards – was not to be deterred. He laid out ornamental gardens and arbours round his 'excellent steel waters' and crowds flocked to see the contortionists and acrobats who performed there. Mr Sadler was indeed lucky for the waters stopped for a time, but by then the crowds were coming mainly for the entertainment!

Sadler's Wells Theatre

Sadler's Wells Theatre, with its long tradition of entertainment, is now looking for a new role; the opera company which took its name moved to the Coliseum in 1968; and the ballet company

Sadler's Wells Theatre

went to Covent Garden – the senior company in 1946 and the junior company in 1957 – to form the Royal Ballet.

Rosoman built the first brick theatre here in 1765 and theatre-goers were escorted by link-boys with flaming torches to avoid the footpads. Winifred Jenkins in Smollett's *Humphry Clinker* (1771) was quite overcome by the 'firing of pistols in the air and blowing of trumpets and singing, and rolling of wheelbarrows on a wire (God bliss us!) no thicker than a sewing thread; that to be sure they must deal with the Devil'. Of the performers towards the end of the eighteenth century Joey Grimaldi, son of 'Iron Legs' Grimaldi, ballet master at Drury Lane, was to become the most famous of clowns. In 1800 he was the first to wear the multi-coloured costume, now traditional, instead of the outré livery; and to paint red half-moons on his cheeks. In 1807 some eighteen

Hogarth's 'Evening'

Joey Grimaldi in 1763 with his father, Giuseppe, who was then ballet master at Sadler's Wells

people were killed after a panic cry of 'fight' was heard as 'fire' by the audience; Grimaldi returned to the theatre by swimming across the New River to find some of those he had been exciting to shouts of laughter a few hours earlier lying dead. Grimaldi, who made thousands laugh before he retired in 1828, is buried in St James's churchyard, Pentonville Road, where his grave with its simple headstone and red rosebush is to this day a pilgrimage for clowns and actors.

In 1802 Charles Dibdin, the younger, and his brother Thomas

became part-owners of Sadler's Wells, and they wrote plays and songs for the burletta house it then became – as did their father, Charles Dibdin the elder. Dibdin showed a spectacular aquatic show with the tank filled up with water from the New River. The Siege of Gibraltar performed by model ships received a thundering applause from the audience; 'and when the ships sailed down, in regular succession "rolling on their way", their sails shifting to the wind; their colours and pennants flying; and their ordnance, as they passed the front of the stage firing a grand salute to the Audience, the latter seemed in an exstacy'. The Duke of Clarence, later William IV, the Sailor King, gave his patronage to the theatre, though some say that his interest may have been encouraged by the fact that Mrs Bland, a sister-in-law of his mistress Mrs Jordan, sang there! But Mary Lamb, writing to Dorothy Wordsworth in 1803, thought Sadler's Wells 'the lowest and most London-like of all our London amusements – the entertainments were Goody Two Shoes, Jack the Giant Killer, and Mary of Buttermere!'

Samuel Phelps – Actor-Manager

Samuel Phelps (1804–78), whose house in Canonbury Square is denoted by a plaque, became manager in 1844, and for the next eighteen years the theatre was renowned for his productions of more than thirty of Shakespeare's plays. Phelps – probably the most versatile actor the English stage ever produced – 'had a meagre figure, his abstemiousness gave him an elasticity of gait and a singular youthfulness. His hands were large-boned, gnarled and even ugly, but eloquently expressive, like his every muscle. His voice (originally weak and piping) was resonant on every word'. He kept the old custom of playing tragedy on a green-baize carpet which Clement Scott, the drama critic, remarked 'was calculated to give the young playgoer a shudder . . . the fatal green baize would sooner or later be strewn with corpses'. Each play, even *Hamlet*, was followed by an operetta, farce or pantomime.

Opera and Ballet under Lilian Bayliss

After being a music hall, and cinema, 'that poor wounded old

MR PHELPS AS HAMLET.

Samuel Phelps, the tragedian

playhouse' was rescued by Lilian Bayliss, who had run the Old Vic first for her aunt and then for herself. The new Sadler's Wells, designed by F. G. Chancellor and built under the architect Frank Matcham & Co., opened on Twelfth Night, 1931, with Shakespeare's play of that name. John Gielgud, who was one of the cast, later recorded: 'How we all detested Sadler's Wells when it was opened first. The auditorium looked like a denuded wedding-cake, and the acoustics were dreadful.' But here in time ballet and opera (sung in English) were to make their home; Markova, aided by Ninette de Valois and others, created the Sadler's Wells Ballet, and musicians such as Benjamin Britten, whose first opera *Peter Grimes* was performed at the theatre after the Second World War, helped establish opera at the theatre.

SPA FIELDS CHAPEL

The Countess of Huntingdon took over the rotunda of the bank-rupted Pantheon tea-gardens in 1779 and converted the building to Spa Fields Chapel for her Methodist Connection to use. The vicar of Clerkenwell, the Reverend William Sellon, however, silenced the ministers there by taking them to the Ecclesiastical Court for preaching without a licence from him. Although the Countess lived in the house next to the chapel which she claimed as hers by right of her peerage, the Court said the ministers must give up their connection either with the chapel or with the Church of England. Two of them seceded from the Church of England while another two gave up preaching at the chapel. The Countess (who had opened various chapels for the Rev. George Whitefield) was an early Methodist, and died at Spa Fields in 1791. The church of Holy Redeemer in Exmouth Market replaced the chapel in 1888 as a Church of England place of worship. Its brick front, with round-arched doorway and rose-window, and its square bell-tower, is clearly Italian in influence. Inside, giant white Corinthian columns set in pale yellow walls support the vaulted blue ceiling. The Stations of the Cross are art nouveau in style; the altar, on the pattern of Sto Spirito in Florence, is under a huge ciborium, and the organ at one time belonged to the Prince Consort. This design by J. D. Sedding, completed by H. Wilson, reminded Walter Pater of the Renaissance churches in Venice.

MOUNT PLEASANT

More than three thousand postal workers sort letters in shifts round the clock every day at Mount Pleasant Post Office where the main sorting office covers three acres. Under this building of 1934 a small underground railway takes the mail to Paddington and Liverpool Street stations. On the site of the Post Office, at the corner of Rosebery Avenue and King's Cross Road, stood the Middlesex House of Correction from 1794 until 1886. This prison was run on lines suggested by John Howard, the great prison reformer, with solitary cells. The severity of the treadmill (introduced in 1822) and the silent system (1834) were still to come. But in 1799 Coleridge commented in *The Devil's Thoughts:*

> *As he went through the Cold-Bath Fields he saw*
> *A solitary cell;*
> *And the Devil was pleased, for it gave him a hint*
> *For improving his prisons in Hell.*

Thistlewood and his fellow Cato Street conspirators, who had plotted to murder the Cabinet, were imprisoned here in 1820; and Leigh Hunt's brother John was confined for libelling the Prince Regent.

FINSBURY TOWN HALL

Finsbury town hall, with its chimneys, turrets and Tudor windows, offers an interesting facade from many viewpoints; this building, on a triangular site facing Rosebery Avenue, was built in 1895 as Clerkenwell's vestry hall; the cream and green hall inside, with boudoir mirrors and angels flourishing electric candelabras, is pure art nouveau.

CITY UNIVERSITY

The former Northampton Institute building facing St John Street is now part of the City University complex which stretches eastwards towards Northampton Square. The design of 1896 by Mountford, the architect of the Old Bailey, lost some of its flourish when part of the roof was flattened; but the main front is still interesting with its richly carved figure-frieze. Northampton House, the home of the Earl of Northampton for a brief period after the Restoration, was on the site of the Institute. During the eighteenth century Richard Brothers, the mad prophet who claimed to be 'a nephew of the Almighty', was committed to the private asylum the building then was.

NEW RIVER AND LLOYD BAKER ESTATES

The New River Company and Lloyd Baker estates north-west of Rosebery Avenue were laid out from the 1820s onwards. Like Canonbury, these estates have remained largely intact through staying in single ownership. The quiet elegant terraces and squares have a unity and simplicity which Bloomsbury must once have had. James Stevens Curl found 'Dutch echoes in the tall windows in brick terraces and high, thin houses with steps up to modestly ornate doorways'.

The New River estate, laid out by William Chadwell Mylne, centres round the church of St Mark, 'of plain Gothic character', which he also designed. To the north of Myddelton Square (1827) lies Claremont Square (1820–45) laid out round the open reservoir of the New River Company. It was covered over in 1856. Thomas Carlyle visited his friend Edward Irving who lived in the east terrace in 1824, and in his *Reminiscences* he recalled that 'it was a new place, houses bright and smart, but inwardly bad as usual'. Amwell Street slopes to the south, and, like a village high street, has its baker, greengrocer, dairy, newsagent, doctor, chemist and undertaker clustered in the centre. Here George Cruikshank the caricaturist lived for a time and drew 'The March of Bricks and Mortar' in 1829. The Clerkenwell Parochial School moved to the Tudor-style building by William Chadwell Mylne in 1828; and further down is the Roman Catholic church of St Peter and St Paul with its Italianate front by John Blyth. It was originally built for the Countess of Huntingdon's Connection.

The Lloyd Baker estate was laid out by John Booth on a site sloping westwards. His son, William Joseph Booth, probably helped. He was later Surveyor to the Drapers' Company in Londonderry who developed much of Draperstown and Moneymore. The houses in Lloyd Square, and Lloyd Baker and Wharton

Streets which slope away westwards, are grouped in pairs with interesting pediments and recessed porches. Between the streets lies Granville Square; the church in the centre 'bearing a massive cross' which featured in Arnold Bennett's novel *Riceyman Steps* was demolished in 1936; but the steps, which used to be called Granville Steps, remain, leading to King's Cross Road. The estate was laid out on land which descended to the Lloyd Baker family from the Backhouse family. They owned the 'Hilly field' and others here in the sixteenth century. Thomas John Lloyd Baker developed the Clerkenwell estate in the early nineteenth century; his father, the Reverend William Lloyd Baker, who was the first to use the surname in its present form, had married a cousin, Mary Lloyd, who became heiress to the Lloyd estates. Mary Lloyd was a great-grand-daughter of William Lloyd, who was Bishop of St Asaph, Lichfield and Worcester successively, and one of the seven bishops sent to the Tower of London by James II on charges of seditious libel. From parts of the Lloyd Baker estate there are magnificent views to the west. On a tri-angular site below Pentonville Road is the stark concrete Weston Rise council estate by Howell, Killick, Partridge and Amis. This was built in 1963 with maisonettes arranged on the scissors principle; the buildings have a dramatic impact difficult to escape from, though many think them forbidding.

III

Canonbury

HISTORY

THE fashionable district of Canonbury is much the same in area
as the manor given by Ralph de Berners to the Prior and Canons
of St Bartholomew in 1253. These Canons who built their country
retreat on the site of Canonbury Tower gave the district its name.
After the dissolution of the monasteries in 1536, Sir John Spencer,
sometime Lord Mayor of London, had his country house here.
This Elizabethan mansion was the place from which, according to
tradition, the first Earl of Northampton carried off Eliza Spencer,
hidden in a baker's basket. On her father's death the estate passed
to the Northampton family; nowadays the Marquess of
Northampton owns only a small part, around the former Canonbury House. During the eighteenth century the fields of Canonbury were popular walks for artists or authors such as Oliver
Goldsmith, who had his lodgings at Canonbury House. The
village of Islington, which ran south to a tip at Islington Green,
extended northwards in the nineteenth century when the
Northamptons laid out Canonbury in elegant terraces and squares.
The parish church of St Mary had been rebuilt in 1751; other
churches such as St Paul's, Ball's Pond Road (by Charles Barry),
and St Stephen's, Canonbury Road (by Inwood and Clifton),
were built in the early nineteenth century for increasing congregations, at a time when church-going for all was as much part
of a Sunday as newspapers are today. Like other parts of Islington,
Canonbury became less fashionable at the turn of the century and
declined; but like a fading prima donna, the estate had its following among writers, intellectuals and artists who appreciated its
'undoubted architectural and aesthetic merits'. The houses kept,

as Sir Milner Holland pointed out, 'the elegance of their period, still discernible even at the district's lowest ebb'.

Something of Canonbury's former rural appeal remains in the trees of Willowbridge Road. In the heart of Canonbury is the basin of the New River, now the haunt of ducks, alongside the willow walk, a country cameo fit for any Wedgwood dinner service. Like the Lloyd Baker estate in Finsbury, the Canonbury estate has benefited from the paternalistic ownership of one family for generations. After the Second World War there was a time when the Canonbury code became the most sought-after on Islington's telephone dials! Since the 1960s neat neo-Georgian terraces, with roses or clematis round some of their doorways, have complemented the existing blocks of nineteenth-century villas and terraces.

Within the triangular boundaries of Canonbury are Islington's town hall (1925), the central fire station and police station, and the parish church of St Mary, all bordering Upper Street, the main road through Islington. With this main road, Essex Road forms the southern point of the area at Islington Green while St Paul's Road marks the northern boundary. The ward of Canonbury includes a triangle of mid-Victorian terraces and twentieth-century council housing bounded by Essex Road, the New North Road and Southgate Road. In this neighbourhood, John Perkins opened a forerunner of the Caledonian market on fifteen acres of land in 1836; he spent about £100,000 in his attempt to lure the cattle traders from Smithfield, but the market flopped!

THE CANONS' HOUSE

The square red-brick Canonbury Tower, about sixty-six feet high, is thought by some to be all that remains of the country retreat that Prior Bolt built; though this is questionable since towards the end of the sixteenth century Sir John Spencer rebuilt most of Canonbury House, and John Dawes added the bay windows to the tower in 1770. Bolton, who was Prior from 1509 to 1532, also restored the priory and church near Smithfield. He left his building mark in many places; one is still visible in a summer house, now part of 4 Alwyne Villas. Bolton's mark was a pun on his name, being formed from a 'bolt', or arrow, and a 'tun', or barrel. The house at Canonbury formed a courtyard along the line of Canonbury Place and seems to have replaced an earlier one, as Stow comments that Bolton 'builded of new the manor of Canonbury at Islington, which belonged to the Canons of that house'.

Canonbury House after the Dissolution

When the monasteries were dissolved, this house with its fish-pond and kitchen gardens came into Henry VIII's possession. The King gave the manor and the adjoining one of Highbury to Thomas Cromwell who had served him so well in the dissolution, and in recommending Anne of Cleves as Queen – or so it seemed at the time. For, within a few months the King had divorced Anne of Cleves, and Thomas Cromwell, newly created Earl of Essex, had been beheaded. Anne of Cleves drew about twenty pounds in alimony 'de manerio nostro de Canberye' which her sponsor had hardly had time to enjoy. Bolton's country house and surrounding gardens passed to John Dudley, Earl of Warwick, in 1547. Warwick held land in Stoke Newington and was astute enough to give Canonbury back to Edward VI, who eventually restored it to him, and created him Duke of Northumberland. After Edward's death, Northumberland tried to make his daughter-in-law, Lady Jane Grey, Queen of England; and was executed by Queen Mary shortly afterwards. She gave Canonbury to her favourite, Thomas Lord Wentworth, who sold the manor in 1570 for £2,000 to 'rich' Spencer.

John Spencer's Canonbury House

John Spencer was so rich that he could easily afford Canonbury. Thirteen pirates from Dunkirk are said to have wanted to kidnap him for a ransom of £50,000; seven came as far as Islington, and there hid themselves in ditches, near the path by which Sir John always came to his house; but, by the providence of God, Sir John was forced to stay in London that night, otherwise they would have taken him away. His town house was Crosby House in Bishopsgate – the great hall of which was moved to Chelsea embankment – formerly the residence of Richard III when he was Duke of Gloucester. Spencer lived there as Lord Mayor of London and entertained in splendour such guests as the Duke of Sully, the French ambassador. Spencer, a clothworker from Suffolk, has left some traces of his wealth in Canonbury. The sumptuous oak carving in the Compton and Spencer rooms in the tower are his; so are the fine ceilings, some of which bear the date 1599, in the east range of buildings, now a day nursery and medical mission. Canonbury House as he rebuilt it had, according to a Venetian contemporary, 'long porticoes or halls without chambers, with windows on each side looking on gardens or rivers, the ceiling being marvellously wrought in stone with gold and the wainscott of carved wood representing a thousand beautiful figures'.

Spencer's Heiress

As in a classic pantomime, 'rich' Spencer had one daughter, Eliza, who was being wooed by one of his neighbours, Lord Compton, an extravagant young nobleman of whom he disapproved. But public opinion and, some said, the Queen were on the side of Lord Compton, and Spencer was 'committed to the Fleet for a contempt, and hiding away his daughter, who, they say, is contracted to Lord Compton; but now he is out again, and by all means seekes to hinder the match, alledging a precontract to Sir Arthur Henningham's sonne. But upon his beating and misusing her, she was sequestered to one Barkers a proctor, and from thence to Sir Henry Billingsleyes, where yet she remaines, till the matter be tried. If the obstinate and self-willed fellow shold persist in his doggednes (as he protests he will) and geve her nothing, the poore Lord shold have a warme catch.'

Elizabeth Spencer's 'Elopement'

As a last resort against Lord Compton's wooing, Elizabeth Spencer is said to have been imprisoned in Canonbury Tower by her father, from where she eloped hidden in a baker's basket carried by Compton, who was disguised as a baker's boy. Spencer, or so it is said, met the 'baker's boy' on the stairs and was so impressed with industry at such an early hour that he tipped him. They were married within the month in 1599 at the church of St

Catharine Colman, Fenchurch Street, 'being thrice asked in the church'. Eventually the couple were reconciled to Spencer apparently by Queen Elizabeth herself who asked him to stand sponsor with her 'to the first offspring of a young couple, happy in their love, but discarded by their father'. The reconciliation was complete with the birth of Lady Compton's daughter at Canonbury House. On Spencer's death in 1609 the fortune passed to Compton who was 'in great danger to loose his witts' and later 'so franticke that he is forced to be kept bound'. He recovered, however, and spent 'within lesses than eight weekes . . . £72,000, most in great horses, rich saddles and playe'.[5] In 1618 he rode from Salisbury House in the Strand for his installation as Knight of the Garter at Windsor Castle with such a brilliant cortège of nearly a hundred followers that the Chapter of the Order gave him a special vote of thanks!

Eliza Compton's 'Housekeeping'

Eliza Compton seemed more modest than her husband. In a letter to him, probably written in 1617, she asks

My sweet Life,

Now I have declared to you my mind for the settling of your state, I suppose that it were best for me to bethink or consider with myself what allowance were meetest for me. For, considering what care I have had of your estate, and how respectfully I dealt with those, which, both by the laws of God, of nature, and of civil polity, wit, religion, government, and honesty, you, my dear, are bound to, I pray and beseech you to grant me £1600 per annum, quarterly to be paid.

Also, I would (besides that allowance for my apparel) have £600 added yearly (quarterly to be paid) for the performance of charitable works, and those things I would not, neither will be accountable for.

Also I will have three horses for my own saddle, that none shall dare to lend or borrow; none lend but I, none borrow but you.

Also, I would have two gentlewomen, lest one should be sick, or have some other lett; also, believe that it is an undecent thing for a gentlewoman to stand mumping alone, when

God hath blessed their lord and lady with a good estate . . .

Also, I will have six or eight gentlemen: and I will have my two coaches, one lined with velvet to myself, with four very fair horses; and a coach for my women, lined with sweet cloth, one laced with gold, the other with scarlet, and laced with watched lace and silver, with four good horses.

Also, I will have two coachmen, one for my own coach, the other for my women . . .

And for myself, besides my yearly allowance, I would have twenty gowns of apparel, six of them excellent good ones, eight of them for the country, and six other of them very excellent good ones.

Also, I would have, to put in my purse, £2,000 and £200; and so for you to pay my debts.

Also, I would have £6,000 to buy me jewels, and £4,000 to buy me a pearl chain.

Now, seeing I am so *reasonable* unto you, I pray you to find my children apparel and their schooling; and also my servants (men and women) their wages . . .

So now that I have declared to you what I would have, and what that is that I would not have, I pray, that when you be an earl, to allow me £1,000 more than I now desire, and *double attendance.*

> Your loving wife,
> Eliza Compton

Dawes' Canonbury House

In 1770 John Dawes, an enterprising stockbroker who later built Highbury House, built a villa (Canonbury House), south of the tower block, and the houses in Canonbury Place. These still stand, with Corinthian pillars at the west end; a brass nameplate in Canonbury Place indicates the home and offices of Sir Basil Spence, architect of Coventry Cathedral; from 1891 to 1899 Weedon Grossmith who wrote *Diary of a Nobody* lived at no. 5 together with his brother.

'Lodgers' at Canonbury House

During the eighteenth century Canonbury Tower was let off in rooms, mainly to writers. The Northamptons had not lived in

1750 print of Canonbury House from the south-west

the house since the Restoration; in 1616 they let the house to Francis Bacon (then Attorney-General): the Latin hexameters of the Kings of England up to Charles I 'who reigned a long time' were inscribed in the tower about this time. Oliver Goldsmith, somewhat short of money, had lodgings in Canonbury Tower, probably to be near John Newbery, the bookseller who was the first to publish little books for children. Goldsmith is said to have finished *The Vicar of Wakefield* here; and he took his 'shoemaker's holidays', never exceeding a crown on dinner at Highbury Barn, tea at White Conduit House and supper at the Grecian or Temple coffee-houses. James Boswell noted in his journal on Sunday, 26 June 1763, 'I then walked out to Islington to Canonbury House, a curious old monastic building

Canonbury Tower today

now let out in lodgings where Dr Goldsmith stays. I took tea with him and found him very chatty.' Arthur Onslow (1691–1768), Speaker of the House of Commons for more than thirty years, went to Canonbury for the 'benefit of the air'. Ephraim Chambers, who published his cyclopaedia in two volumes in 1728, died at Canonbury in 1740; he used to take rooms at Canonbury House as 'his close and unremitting attention to his studies' affected his health. Washington Irving, the American writer who created Rip van Winkle, took Goldsmith's room for a few days in the early nineteenth century. His 'intolerable landlady', however, kept taking parties round the tower and showing them Goldsmith's room where he was working. When he locked the door to keep them out, she let the visitors peep through the keyhole at 'the author who was always in a tantrum when interrupted'. Irving was annoyed and wrote: 'I could not open my window lest I was stunned with shouts and noises from the cricket ground, the late quiet road beneath my window was alive with the tread of feet and the clack of tongues; and, to complete my misery, I found that my quiet retreat was absolutely a "show house", the tower and its contents being shown to strangers at sixpence a head . . . So I bade adieu to Canonbury Castle, Merry Islington, and the haunts of poor Goldsmith without having advanced a single line in my labours.'

Tower Theatre

In 1907 the fifth Marquess of Northampton restored the tower where the bailiff of the estate had lived since 1826. The ivy was removed; iron railings round the top of the tower were replaced by a brick parapet; some of the old oak roofbeams were used for restoration. He built King Edward's Hall, now the Tower Theatre, as a recreation hall for the tenants of his Canonbury and Clerkenwell estates. The building was converted into a theatre in 1952 by the Tavistock Repertory Company which had moved from Tavistock Place, Bloomsbury; it had originated there as an amateur repertory company, part of the Mary Ward Settlement.

FOWLER'S ELIZABETHAN MANSION

To the south of Canonbury House, which until the early nineteenth century was surrounded by fields intersected by paths, stood the Elizabethan mansion of Sir Thomas Fowler, Lord of the Manor of Barnsbury, on the site of the present Cross Street Baptist Church. Fowler was a deputy-lieutenant for the county of Middlesex, and a juror at the trial of Sir Walter Raleigh at Winchester in 1603. The ceilings in his mansion were comparable to those in Canonbury House and at the northern end of the garden was a summer-house or porter's lodge 'absurdly called Queen Elizabeth's lodge'. As Nelson points out, the 'situation must have afforded a pleasant and agreeable retreat, enjoying a prospect of the fine mansion and park of Canonbury, with the woods of Highbury on the one side, and the village church, with a few scattered houses, and an open view over the fields towards the metropolis, on the other'.

CANONBURY SQUARE

Early in the nineteenth century, building began in earnest with Canonbury Square, still much the same as when completed in

Canonbury Square from the north side

1826, though the north-east side has been restored since the Second World War. The New North Road, which was built at the same time to provide a better route to the City, bisects the square as Canonbury Road; as this traffic moves directly through the square and not round the gardens in the centre, much of the feeling of an urban cloister is lost. The houses are as fine as many in Bloomsbury squares: those on the south-west side are definitely by Leroux, though the whole square is also attributed to him. Samuel Phelps (as a plaque shows) lived in this terrace set back from the road with a high pavement, he was responsible for a golden Shakespearean epoch at Sadler's Wells, which he managed from 1844 to 1862. Joseph Chamberlain went to a prep school in the square before going to University College School; Evelyn Waugh published *Decline and Fall* and *Vile Bodies* while living there in the 1920s; Vanessa Bell and Duncan Grant were attracted by it; and in 1945, Eric Blair, who published his biting satire *Animal Farm* the same year under the name of George Orwell, lived in a flat in one of the houses.

COMPTON TERRACE

When Leroux first designed Compton Terrace in the early nineteenth century, the nonconformist Union chapel harmonized with its neighbours. By 1876, however, the Victorian Congregationalists needed a larger chapel to seat their growing numbers – at one time the organist had some two hundred pupils for singing lessons – and so the gigantic red-brick chapel displaced the terrace chapel. This 'Gothic tornado,' in the words of Elizabeth and Wayland Young, remains a monument to Victorian Congregationalism; but its sheet bulk, like that of St John the Evangelist church in Duncan Terrace, mars this fine terrace, set back from Islington's main road with a classical linear park.

POST WAR BUILDING

North of Canonbury Tower are neo-Georgian squares and terraces, with communal lawns in front, still trim and new. In Canonbury Park North and Canonbury Park South there are a few houses by Louis de Soissons, the architect largely associated with Welwyn Garden City, whose scheme for redeveloping parts of Canonbury after the Second World War was not used. The huge pairs of villas known as the Alwynes still stand after a scheme to replace them with modern flats has been abandoned. As a result of pressure from conservationists, the Government introduced a Bill to ensure that buildings vital to the character of a conservation area are safeguarded. On some 28 acres east of the New River Walk, the squares and mews streets form a pedestrian enclave in the Marquess Road housing scheme, built at a cost of more than £5 million and designed by Darbourne and Darke.

CANONBURY TAVERN AND ALMEIDA STREET

At Canonbury Tavern the inhabitants of Islington met in 1803 during the threat of the Napoleonic wars to re-form the Loyal Islington Volunteers. Later, in 1832, an Islington literary society was formed at the tavern which had been popular with its tea-gardens and bowling green. The members of the Islington Literary and Scientific Institution met from 1837 to 1878 at their head-quarters in Almeida Street, Barnsbury, designed by Gough and Roumieu, and used by Beck's Carnival Novelties until recently as a warehouse. Here in the theatre the members had lectures and saw an Egyptian mummy unrolled in 1840; there was a museum, library, laboratory and apparatus rooms.

CHURCHES

To the north is St Paul's church which was nearly built as a replica of St John's church, Holloway, but both Charles Barry and the parishioners objected. A compromise was reached by putting the tower at the east entrance; as a result a vault was formed behind the altar giving the impression of a gallery over-looking it. This was commonly known as 'The Marquess's pew' – but though the site in Ball's Pond Road was given by the Marquess of Northampton in 1828, it has, needless to say, never been a pew! To the south is St Stephen's church in Canonbury Road built in 1837 with a spire said to be modelled on St Mary's church, Oxford. The church was lengthened in 1850 by A. D. Gough, only to be shortened more than a century later in 1957 by A. Llewellyn Smith and A. W. Waters in their post war restoration. The New River no longer flows through Canonbury, but its basin now forms part of the New River Walk opened in 1954 by the Labour statesman, Herbert Morrison, later Lord Morrison of Lambeth.

St Mary's Parish Church

The spire of St Mary's church in Upper Street has been part of the skyline of Islington since 1754; Lancelot Dowbiggin, who does not seem to have designed any other churches, made this graceful spire a combination of what he considered the three 'handsomest churches in London' – St Bride's, Bow and Shoreditch. In 1787 hundreds flocked to see the spire enclosed, rather like a beehive, in wickerwork scaffolding; this wickerwork, (formed entirely of willow, hazel and other sticks by Thomas Birch, a basket-maker), was built to fix a lightning conductor. The spiral staircase which ran round the spire was said to be as 'easy and safe as the stairs of a dwelling house'. Birch made more money from the sightseers who paid sixpence a time than from his commission! The rest of Dowbiggin's church was destroyed during the Second World War; Lord Mottistone and Paul Paget restored the building largely according to the eighteenth-century box-like plan, but the interior is modern with murals on the east and west walls by Brian Thomas. The churchyard with a sexton's house of the 1740s is now a public garden; a few tombstones remain, among which is the carefully tended vault of Richard Cloudesley, who gave the Stonefields estate to the parish in 1517, asking that thirty requiem masses a year should be said for the repose of his soul for ever. There is a legend that all these provisions made by Cloudesley were in vain as there were minor earthquakes or 'tremblements de terre' in fields near his tomb; and 'certaine exorcisers . . . did at dede of night . . . using divers divine exercises at torche light, set at rest ye unrulie spirit of ye sayde Cloudesley, and ye earthe did returne aneare to its pristine shape'. Sir George Wharton and James Steward, a godson of James I, who both served the King, were buried here in one grave at his wish after killing each other in a duel near Islington. Rumour has it that Hannah Lightfoot, the Quakeress who bore George III a daughter and is said to have married him, was buried here under the name of Rebecca Powell. In this churchyard George Whitefield preached in 1739 after a church warden had forbidden him the pulpit within the church; the sermon this early Methodist delivered from a tomb-stone was such that the listeners could have gone even to prison

The spire of St Mary's church enclosed in wickerwork scaffolding

singing hymns. But the sermon led to the banning of the Wesleys and Whitefield from both church and churchyard by the church-wardens; and the Reverend George Stonehouse, who had intro-duced them, resigned his living.

EVANGELISM AND MARTYRS

The vicarage of St Mary's was built by W. H. Barlow, designer of the roof of St Pancras station, and a brother of Dr William Hagger Barlow who had been principal of the Church Missionary Society College before being appointed vicar in 1886. In the Memorial Hall next door (1890) the Islington Clerical Meeting was held for a time, later to grow into the Islington Conference for Evangelicals.

The Reverend Daniel Wilson, who was vicar from 1824 to 1832, started the Islington Clerical Meeting in his vicarage in Barnsbury Park. He had been given the patronage of the living by his father-in-law, which at the time included two shillings an acre for arable land, 4d an acre for pasture, 2d per cow, and 2d per calf. When Wilson became Bishop of Calcutta, his son, the Reverend Daniel Wilson II, succeeded him as vicar. He carried on his father's evangelical work, and when Bishop Blomfield ordered the vicars of the eleven parishes in Islington in 1842 to preach in their surplices, they refused and he was forced to withdraw his direction. But unlike some of those who refused to obey Mary Tudor's orders to attend the parish church, they were not burned at the stake. In 1557 John Rough, who was a friend of John Knox, the Scottish reformer, met with others at the Saracen's Head, pretending to hear a play, while they wor-shipped in a protestant manner. They were betrayed by a tailor and arrested; a year later forty men and women who met secretly in 'a back close in the field by the town of Islington' were also betrayed. Of these, thirteen were burned at the stake following the fate of the other Islington martyrs, John Rough and three men and a woman.

THE LITTLE ANGEL

In the Dickensian alley of Dagmar Passage is the Little Angel Theatre run by John Wright as a permanent puppet theatre since

The Martyrdom of Ralph Allerton, Jam.ˢ Austoo, Margery Austoo and Richard Roth, at Islington, 1557.

Islington martyrs burnt at the stake

1961; children now crowd into the hall which was once the meeting place of teetotallers who belonged to Henry Ansell's Good Templar Lodge.

In Cross Street which slopes eastwards are eighteenth-century houses as fine as some in Bath; the doorways of Nos. 33 and 35, as Sir John Summerson has pointed out, are imitations of the Adams' Adelphi.

In Essex Road the south-east branch library (1916) by Mervyn Macartney, a member of the 'Norman Shaw' school of architecture, and the neo-Egyptian front of the former ABC cinema (now a Bingo club), opened in 1930 by Prince Arthur of Connaught, are rare examples of early twentieth-century architecture in Islington

COLLINS' MUSIC HALL

From 1862 until 1958 Collins' Music Hall faced Islington Green. Sam Vagg, a chimney sweep who had made his name on the stage as Sam Collins, turned the Lansdowne Arms into a music hall; he was known for his Irish songs, such as *The Rocky Road*

Collins' Music Hall, 1959, by G. S. Fletcher

to Dublin and *Limerick Races*. At the age of thirty-nine, three years after opening Collins', known in the 1870s as the 'little gold mine', Sam Vagg died. Among those billed at the 'chapel-on-the-green' (the gags at one time were so clean) were Marie Lloyd, George Robey, Harry Lauder, Gracie Fields, Charlie Chaplin, Norman Wisdom and Tommy Trinder. Sickert came night after night to study the performers in the music hall which had been rebuilt in 1897; and in the bar was a famous collection of old playbills and autographed photographs of music-hall stars which was sold when the building was demolished in 1963; a plaque now marks its site.

IV

St Peter's

The fields of St Peter's formed the rump of the Prebend manor which William the Conqueror restored to the Canons of St Paul. They had held all Islington before the land passed into the hands of the Berners family and the Knights of St John. Lewis records: 'As the corps of one of the prebends of St Paul's, it is called, in old records, *Iseldon extra London.* The prebendal stall in the cathedral is the eleventh on the north side of the choir, and is inscribed, '*Islington. In Convertendo Dom. Capt.*'. It is rated in the king's books at £11 10s. 10d. and is taxed at eight marks.' In the eighteenth century when the first building of terraces such as Duncan Terrace began in Islington, the area consisted of fields and nursery gardens with an odd inn such as The Old Queen's Head and the Barley Mow. The district of St Peter's took its name from the church designed in 1835 by Sir Charles Barry which still stands in the street of the same name. Part of the Regent's Canal was cut through this area in the early nineteenth century, where Sir Hugh Myddleton's New River also ran down to Clerkenwell. As in other parts of Islington, some of the fields were used as brickfields before terraces of Victorian houses were built here.

CHARACTER

St Peter's Street, which bisects the ward of St Peter's, was formerly River Lane. It changes its character completely as it runs across the Regent's Canal past the curious north-west tower of St Peter's church and narrows at its Essex Road end into a neo-

St Peter's church, River Lane, *c.* 1835

Italian alley. The church by Charles Barry, first known as St Peter's in the Brickfields, was built for little more than £3,000. Clarke states: 'It deserves to be called a brick box, and the style is pitiably mean Early English.' Thomas Cromwell thought the building a plain and neat chapel – but this was before the embellishments were added by Gough and Roumieu in 1843 to plans approved by Barry.

The backs of Noel Road and Vincent Terrace overlook the Regent's Canal and this part is reminiscent of Little Venice in Paddington. In the City Basin, hemmed in by warehouses, youngsters now take to the water with the Islington Boat Club. Through the island-like locks the narrow pleasure boats carry Londoners along this man-made waterway where barge after barge tugged by horses once made its way to the docks. Walter Sickert drew the inspiration for his engraving, 'Hanging Gardens of Islington', from the canal bank. Duncan Terrace, named after the admiral who distinguished himself at Cape St Vincent, formerly overlooked the New River flowing towards Clerkenwell. So did the opposite terrace, Colebrooke Row, most probably

Sickert's engraving: 'The Hanging Gardens of Islington'

named after James Colebrooke, the largest landowner in the parish of St Mary at the time; he was given the honour of laying the foundation stone of the new parish church in 1751. The New River was covered over in 1861 and the grandeur of these town houses is no longer mirrored in its waters. In 1890 New Terrace, Camden and Colebrooke Terraces were incorporated in a renumbered Duncan Terrace. Bridges span the green open spaces of the Packington estate, built on land Dame Anne Packington left in 1559 to benefit the poor. Near the church of St James in Prebend Street, erected by the Clothworkers' Company, their almshouses still stand. Camden Passage, which runs parallel to Upper Street, is an antique market precinct nowadays; on market days this popular market becomes as crowded as a film set.

The New North Road to the north, the City Road to the south, Essex Road to the west and the canal to the east form the boundaries of the area.

CAMDEN PASSAGE

Islington High Street runs north between a solid electricity substation and gaunt eighteenth-century houses into the narrow paved precinct of Camden Passage. On market days it seems that nearly all the dealers who had a pitch on the stones of Caledonian Market squeeze their attic treasures into tiny stalls here! 'The passage', as this row of boutiques is known in the trade, spills over into neighbouring arcades which have spread since the 1960s when antique dealers made it their own. Restaurants, such as Robert Carrier's, have attracted sophisticated diners, while the trendy furniture by designers such as Christien Sell have made a meteoric impact on a passage where gleaming mahogany can command its price.

Camden Passage (which incorporated Cumberland Row) was renamed throughout in 1876 after Charles Pratt, the first Earl of Camden and a celebrated eighteenth-century Lord Chancellor. The council housing of Colinsdale (commended by the Civic Trust) is built over Camden Street, and Victorian extravaganza flourishes in the Camden Head, thanks to Robert Gradidge's skilful restoration. Alexander Cruden, once Bookseller to Queen Caroline, died in Camden Passage in 1770, as a plaque shows. In 1737 Cruden, hoping for her patronage, presented the Queen with

Vera Skinner's engraving of Camden Passage

a copy of his *Concordance of the Holy Scriptures*, dedicated to her. She promised to 'remember him' but unfortunately died some days later, leaving Cruden with a book and business beyond his resources. Cruden became insane and was confined to an asylum for various periods; he worked as a proof-reader styling himself 'Alexander the Corrector', and went from place to place rebuking Sabbath-breaking and profanity. He died with his hopes of marrying an heiress, being knighted and becoming a Member of Parliament still illusions.

GRAND THEATRE

From 1860 to 1907 the Philharmonic Hall, and its successor the Grand Theatre, stood on the east side of Islington High Street. Graced by Grecian figures, the tattered façade of the last re-building of this theatre (so bedevilled by numerous fires) is barely recognizable. By the 1870s the Philharmonic Hall, which had opened for 'first class concerts', was vulgarly known as 'the Spittoon'. Charles Morton launched French light operas in 1871 with Emily Soldene, whose smile was described as a melon with a slice taken out! Miss Soldene was also an astute manageress: she brought the troupe of high-kicking can-can girls to the Philharmonic when the Alhambra lost its music-hall licence because of them in 1871. After the hall became the Grand Theatre in 1883, Lottie Collins sang her *Ta-ra-ra-boom-de-ay*, which she had first adapted from a negro minstrel song *Tin-a-ling-a-ling-aboomderary*, at the Tivoli in 1890.

DUNCAN TERRACE

Charlton Place, with a Jane Austen air about its crescented terrace, links Camden Passage with Duncan Terrace; Eduard Suess, founder of the 'new geology' was born here in 1831, as a plaque denotes. The houses with their high pavement in the middle of this terrace, and those at each end of Colebrooke Row, still display their classical Georgian fronts, now mellowed by age. The red-brick twin towers and Norman front of St John the Evangelist church breaks into Duncan Terrace with a Vic-torian brashness rather similar to its Congregational counterpart, the Union chapel, in Compton Terrace. The building, which Pugin thought 'the most original combination of modern deformity that has been erected for some time past', took quite a time to build and was only consecrated in 1873.

Charles Lamb's Cottage

In the 1820s Charles Lamb – at the time a clerk at East India House – came to a cottage (detached in those days) to live the life of a country gentleman. He would watch the setting sun from the top of Canonbury Tower or smoke his pipe in the Old Queen's Head. The New River ran past the front of the house in Duncan Terrace, now denoted by a plaque, and after his friend Dyer had tumbled into it, Lamb dubbed it the 'stream Dyerian'. In 1823 he wrote to Bernard Barton, the Quaker poet, about his cottage: 'A white house, with six good rooms; the New River (rather elderly by this time) runs (if a moderate walking pace may be so termed) close to the foot of the house; and behind is a spacious garden with vines, (I assure you), pears, strawberries, parsnips, leeks, carrots, cabbages, to delight the heart of old Alcinous. You enter without passage into a cheerful dining-room, all studded over and rough with old books: and above is a lightsome drawing-room, three windows, full of choice prints. I feel like a great lord, never having had a house before.' Thomas Hood, the poet and humorist, who visited Lamb, thought the house 'a cottage of ungentility, for it had neither double coach house nor wings. Like its tenant it stood alone.' Lamb, who had written essays under the name of Elia, moved in 1827 to Edmonton with a pension of £441.

STARVATION FARM

Towards the end of the eighteenth century an eccentric Portuguese baron, Ephraim Lopez Pereira D'Aguilar, kept, near Colebrooke Row, a stock of cattle so lean that the place was known as 'Starvation Farm'. The crowds would pelt the baron whenever he appeared to feed the poor animals, who finally died for lack of food. His answer to their jeers was that he did it so his cattle might know their master! In addition, this baron, who had twice married heiresses, kept a household 'of the most abandoned dissoluteness, several females and their families living together

Engraving of Charles Lamb's house in Duncan Terrace

with him at the same time'. As a result he had numerous illegiti-
mate children; when a parish officer sought the usual indemnity
for one of these, he reached for his ledger and remarked how
much greater the demand was than he had been accustomed to
pay before! After his death in 1802 his cattle were sold for £128
and his favourite coach, which was almost dropping to pieces,
for £7 – a trifle in his total estate which exceeded £200,000.

Regent's Canal

Between the luxuriant backs of Noel Road and the railed-off
bank of Vincent Terrace, the Regent's Canal emerges from the
long Islington tunnel. After the collapse of the Archway tunnel
in 1812, the building of the new one was a testing challenge for
Nash's engineer Morgan. This passage, 970 yards long, still
carries the canal as a tribute to his engineering skill, though
certain householders in Chapel Street complained at the time!
In 1820 Lord Macclesfield and his party passed through the

Regent's Canal, Islington

tunnel for the first time in the City state barge, decked out in colourful flags and trimmings. They were greeted at the City Road basin with the firing of a salute while bands played. The competition to land the first produce on the wharf was won by the sailors of the *William* who downed a whole cask of ale they had brought ashore to celebrate! Until 1826 when special tunnel tugs were introduced at Islington, the barges were moved through the passage by three 'leggers', who lay on boards set across the decks and pushed against the walls of the tunnel with their feet. Cromwell stated that the tugs produced a 'Tartarean aspect. The smoke, the fire, and the noise of the engine, uniting with the deep gloom of the arch, the blackness of the water, the crashing of the vessels against the sides of the tunnel and each other, and the lurid light that glimmers beyond each distant extremity, form an aggregate of *infernalia*, that must be witnessed to be adequately conceived'. The barges towed by horses along the canal served the newly built West India docks, the London docks, the Surrey docks and the East India docks.

NOEL ROAD

Sickert had a studio in Noel Road in the 1930s with a large window overlooking the canal. He papered the walls with crimson paper flecked with gold and had comfortable, shabby chairs. To this studio Major Lessore, his brother-in-law, brought the artist's dummy which had belonged to Hogarth; this later inspired Sickert to paint the 'Raising of Lazarus', for which he did the first design on the red wallpaper of his studio in Highbury Place. His impression of the canal-side gardens are depicted in 'The Hanging Gardens of Islington'. In the 1960s, Joe Orton, who wrote successful comedies such as *Loot* and *Entertaining Mr Sloane*, lived here with another writer. In 1962 they were both imprisoned for defacing library books; their flat was papered with pictures of every description. In 1967 they were both found dead; in a grotesque frenzy, Joe Orton had been battered to death by his flat-mate who then committed suicide.

THE OLD QUEEN'S HEAD

South of St Peter's Street, Thomas Cubitt the builder bought five acres known as Hattersfield in 1827, and built six houses in St Peter's Street, the end houses of the terrace being emphasized by a single large balcony instead of two separate ones. William Quilter built the Oxford and Cambridge Terraces in Grantbridge Street in 1855.

The Old Queen's Head on Essex Road is now a modern pub, but the ceilings and the chimney-piece of the Elizabethan inn have been incorporated. This inn was demolished in 1830. Samuel Lewis described it as 'one of the most perfect specimens of ancient domestic architecture in the vicinity of London'. The building, with three lofty storeys projecting over each other in front with bay windows, had a rich interior of oak-panelled wainscots and stuccoed ceilings. The chimney-piece with carved stone figures of Venus, Bacchus and Plenty remains; as does the ceiling ornamented with dolphins, cherubs and acorns. Not surprisingly, the origin of the building was the basis for many pub stories: some said that Sir Walter Raleigh smoked his first pipe there – though the Old Pied Bull in Theberton Street also claims this honour; that the inn sign was a compliment to Queen Elizabeth I; that the house had been the residence of Lord Treasurer Burleigh; and that Elizabeth's favourite, the Earl of Essex, had lived there!

TEA-GARDENS

Towards the end of the eighteenth century George Morland, whose name evokes a nosegay of cottage flowers, painted country subjects at the Barley Mow in Frog Lane, now Popham Road. For the most part devoted to the bottle and the company of his low associates there, he also sketched old cart-harnesses and rustic characters. A path across the fields led eastwards to the Rosemary Branch, originally an ale-house near the windmills of a white lead factory. This became a popular tea-garden stretching over three acres; on its large pond there was boating in the summer and skating in the winter. Owing to 'the total disappearance of the water, through the general drainage of the neighbourhood for the accommodation of the surrounding buildings' the landlord lost his pond and his profits!

ST JAMES'S CHURCH

The church of St James was built in Prebend Street in 1873 at the cost of £10,000 to replace Lambe's chapel in the City. The ragstone building on its island site was designed by Frederick William Porter, architect to the Clothworkers' Company which had its estate here. In a niche over the door inside is a coloured figure, dated 1612, of William Lambe, Master of the Clothworkers. This Company still attends the church once a year and dispenses twenty-four pairs of shoes to pensioners.

PACKINGTON ESTATE

The Packington housing estate was built by Wates on a twelve-acre site after a long planning controversy in the 1960s. Those who opposed the scheme, which provided some 540 flats at a cost of more than £3 million, argued that the Victorian houses then in Packington Street should be renovated instead. Mr Richard Crossman, then Minister of Housing, allowed the redevelopment, but, following a public inquiry, ordered that a revised scheme be adopted by the council. This decision led to further debate.

ISLINGTON FILM STUDIOS

Though actually situated in Shoreditch, the Gainsborough film studios in Poole Street were known as the 'Islington studios'. Michael Balcon and Reginald Baker (an accountant) negotiated for the studios in the early 1920s with Paramount British, who were asking for more than £100,000. Balcon and Baker made a counter offer of £14,000 for the studios in a converted power house, were accepted, and then as they did not have the cash, paid it back on hire purchase! Alfred Hitchcock started in the cutting room at these studios and went on to direct *Downhill*, starring Ivor Novello; George Pearson's Betty Balfour films, *Love, Life and Laughter, Squibs' Honeymoon, Squibs' M.P.*, were made here; and so were the early Ivor Novello's: *The Rat, The Lodger, The Triumph of the Rat, The Vortex, The Constant Nymph* and *Return of the Rat*.

While *Balaclava* (an early version of *The Charge of the Light Brigade*), with Cyril McLagen and Benita Hume was being made, fire destroyed one of the floors and interrupted production at these studios. A run of musical films followed, among which was *Sunshine Susie* with Renate Muller, Jack Hulbert and Owen

Nares, which became a box-office hit. Cicely Courtneidge appeared in musical films such as *Soldiers of the King;* and Margaret Lock-wood made her early films, *Bank Holiday* being but one, at the Islington studios. Balcon's Gainsborough Pictures were first absorbed by Gaumont British and later by Rank. The 'Islington studios' closed down in 1948 and the building became a distillery.

V

Barnsbury and Pentonville

HISTORY

Ralph de Berners, who gave his name to this part of Islington, at one time held the manors both of Barnsbury and Canonbury. Most of the manor of Barnsbury lay to the north of modern Barnsbury in Holloway and formed a tongue in the east of the district as it is now. The fields to the west belonged to the Knights of St John of Jerusalem; eventually the Thornhill family came to own most of this – the street names have connections with the Thornhills who still own an estate here. To the south lies Pentonville, which was one of the first-late eighteenth-century developments to come out of the improved communication of the City Road, built to link the City with Paddington. In the 1820s the Chalk Road, or Caledonian Road as it came to be known, opened a better route to the north; the fields of Barnsbury were used as brickfields and later turned into a variety of squares each with its individualistic stamp. The building of the Agricultural Hall in 1862 for cattle shows seemed apt, following the disappearance of the dairy fields in the area.

CHARACTER

The terraces and squares of Barnsbury form a townscape now blended through age and accident to form a locality rich in variety of styles. The houses in Pentonville were in their time popular with the clerks that Dickens and George du Maurier described in their novels; no doubt they crowded the omnibuses of Shillibeer to commute to the City, or walked from Pentonville to their offices. The area was laid out by Mr Henry Penton towards

C. H. Matthews's watercolour of Barnsbury Moat, 'Roman camp', in 1836

the end of the eighteenth century. Much of it is gone, including the house in Rodney Street where John Stuart Mill learnt Greek at the age of three. The parish church of St James's where the Pentonville bourgeoisie, in their bonnets and hats, flocked on a Sunday, is now merely surrounded by trees. Chapel Street, where Charles Lamb lodged with his sister Mary and householders complained about the tunnelling of the new Regent's Canal, has been turned, since the 1860s, by stall-holders into a bustling fruit and vegetable market.

The north–south axis of Cloudesley and Lonsdale Squares, and of Gibson and Milner Squares, form stately urban land-scapes to delight passers-by. Thornhill Square hugs a large 'country' church in its northern crescent; and Barnsbury Square – with its closes and openings – seems more like a green than a town square. Through this throbs the life of an urban community dependant in part on the small factories, offices and shops for a living. In Thornhill Road with its school, pub, butcher, garage, and small green, a Hampstead village atmosphere seems to be in the making. Anthony Carson, writing in the *New Statesman*, found the heart of this village 'The Rising Sun in Brooksby Street and [the Thornhill Road] runs up past the Albion and then peters off in a grey cloud of brick . . . Around this area are trim houses with owl faces, squares with official and unofficial flowers.' To the west of the Caledonian Road and south of Copenhagen Street some postwar blocks of council housing are grouped into precincts so popular with contemporary planners. The bull-dozers and bombs have destroyed the slums they replace, though some tenemented terraces remain – recalling the glory of the empire in India in such names as Delhi, Outram and Havelock Streets. Barnsbury (including Pentonville) is bounded by Pentonville Road to the south, Upper Street to the east, Offord Road and Laycock Street to the north, and York Way to the west.

EXPERIMENTAL TRAFFIC SCHEME

In the past few years Barnsbury has been the subject of more reports than any other part of Islington; they deal with an experimental traffic scheme introduced in 1970. The problem the authorities faced was how to apply the traffic principles Professor Buchanan had defined in *Traffic and Towns*, to more than a limited area without ignoring the housing needs of the existing community. David Wager, a town-planner and resident at the time, put forward a plan in 1965 to keep Barnsbury as a residential area; he wrote: 'In order to revive its "village" character – and identity as a Living Unit – through traffic must be excluded, and necessarily provided for, by creating proper urban through routes around the boundaries of the area.' An environmental study initiated by Mr Richard Crossman (then Minister of Housing) was made and the findings published in 1968; the Islington Borough Council then introduced an experimental traffic scheme, which became a matter of vigorous debate, mainly between two local pressure groups, the Barnsbury Association and the Barnsbury Action Group. The effect of the scheme is to turn central Barnsbury into a maze only local residents can unravel, thus limiting commuter through traffic.

LIVERPOOL ROAD

Barnsbury (apart from Pentonville) was laid out between 1820 and 1850 though there was earlier ribbon development along Liverpool Road and Upper Street. In Liverpool Road, now a main thoroughfare for lorry drivers from that port and elsewhere, some fine terraces, built on the back road it once was, survive. Cloudesley Terrace seems well shielded by its front gardens and high pavement with railings from a thoroughfare which by-passed Islington village. Park Place, built in 1790, as a stone plaque proudly states, is now defaced with red-brick bow-fronts jutting forwards at odd intervals. Two terraces have been restored by the Greater London Council – Barnsbury Terrace and that between Cloudesley Place and Batchelor Street (which was commended by the Civic Trust). Set anywhere else the Royal Free Hospital might well be mistaken for a small country house; the red-brick, colonnaded façade is Palladian in style and has two wings, and in the forecourt is an Italian fountain. But the Victorians used this to disguise the wards of typhoid and scarlet fever patients, who were admitted to the London Fever Hospital from 1849. This Fever Hospital building became part of the Royal Free Hospital in 1948, and now houses some women's wards and the private wing. In 1862 Charles Dickens described the hospital designed by Charles Fowler as 'not only the single hospital of its kind in London but probably the best hospital of its kind in Europe'.

Square twin towers topped by pavilion ironwork mark the former main entrance of the Agricultural Hall opened in 1862 in Liverpool Road. The vast roof, by Heaviside of Derby, shows Victorian engineering at its best in its 125-foot span. Lord Berners laid the foundation stone of the monstrous two-acre hall for the members of the Smithfield Club to exhibit their cattle. This red-brick forerunner of Olympia cost them £32,000 to build, but for some time there was no problem of space! In 1884 the hall added 'Royal' to its title when Queen Victoria, who had been a frequent and successful exhibitor at its hows, bestowed that accolade. In 1891, she sent a Collie and three Pomeranians to the first dog show run by Charles Cruft in the hall. Cruft, who had been a salesman for James Spratt, organized shows here until his death in 1938.

Exhibitions and Shows

Until the 'Aggie' became a G.P.O. parcels sorting office during the Second World War, thousands crowded the hall for exhibitions and shows of every kind. Queen Victoria attended the Workmen's International Exhibition in 1870 – the same year that a bullfight took place and the Spanish bullfighters were fined £1 each! In the 1870s the American revivalists Sankey and Moody drew crowds and the Mohawk 'burnt-cork nigger' Minstrels appeared. In the 1880s the first military tournament was held in the hall and marathon walking races were all the rage. In the 1890s Charles Blondin walked the tight-rope at the age of seventy as 'nimble and active as ever'.

The Royal Military Tournament had become part of the London season in the hall where the Prince of Wales attended a ball in 1867. The two hundred soldiers' and sailors' orphans from the Royal Caledonian Asylum went through their 'musical drill and dumb-bell exercise with surpassing neatness and the regularity of a mechanical motion', Charles Eyre Pascoe, the writer of a handbook on the London season, wrote; 'The Royal Horse and

The Smithfield Club cattle show at the New Agricultural Hall

Field Artillery batteries give a brilliant display of driving at a trot and gallop, the thundering stride of horses and the roll of guns producing a great impression on the visitors unaccustomed to such spectacles. Then a blare of trumpets heralds the approach of Life Guards, who in all the glory of their accoutrements go through the intricate evolutions of a musical ride with faultless precision. Riding with firm, easy seats, light hands, and stately bearing, these stalwart troopers look the perfection of cavalry soldiers. At a canter their horses "change feet", without pause or break, as they circle right and left, and keep time to the music like skilful dancers in a cotillon. When, having finished, they slowly march out of the arena, the applause that follows them is loud and long.' By Edwardian times Charles Cordingley was organizing early motor shows at the hall, and Mr Glass, who later established his 'Guide', held his first 'Used Motor Show' at the hall in 1916. Though the hall now stands empty and is under the threat of demolition, an active 'Use the Royal Agricultural Hall' campaign is fighting to save it for Islington citizens.

MR GIBSON'S ESTATE

Mr Thomas Milner Gibson, later to become a leading anti-Corn-Law orator and president of the Board of Trade, had his estate in Islington laid out between 1828 and 1846. Theberton Street (with lower-rated houses in Moon Street and Studd Street to the rear) was named after Mr Gibson's country seat in Suffolk, Theberton Hall, and the squares, of course, bore his own names. Gibson Square (*c.* 1832) has two mirror-identical terraces east and west, facing each other; at the ends are pedimented roofs and mock-pillar fronts. In the centre of the square the gardens are restored to a classical formality with iron railings and a neo-classical gazebo one would expect to find as a country-house folly. In fact, this houses a ventilation shaft for the recently built Victoria Line! Robert Carrier, the restaurateur and cookery writer who lived in the square, brought a sophisticated touch to it.

To the north lies Milner Square (*c.* 1841), nearly built as a terrace, which proably would not have aroused so much comment! The individualistic architects Gough and Roumieu designed this narrow square, and the rows of thin arched windows in the oblong houses are reminiscent of a surrealistic painting.

The fronts have been stripped of their balconies and porches which, together with a paved piazza centre, might have brought a touch of Italy to this urban nightmare. Christopher Hussey

Gibson Square

thought that 'though for residential purposes, Milner Square is somewhat gloomy and monotonous owing to its complete sup-pression of the individual unit, there is no denying its impres-siveness'. Sir John Summerson's feeling is that one can visit the square many times and 'still not be absolutely certain that you have seen it anywhere but in an unhappy dream'. He explains that the architects 'attempted here to redeem the Georgian house-front from its negativeness by resolving it into a pattern of vertical *anta*-like ribs with windows and wall-

E

Milner Square

panels in the intervals. The principle is reasonable enough but the mannerisms in the modelling give the design an unreal and tortured quality'.

STONEFIELDS ESTATE

The fourteen acres of the Stonefields estate left by Richard Cloudesley to the parish in 1517 were laid out in the 1820s. More than four centuries after his death he is still remembered in the parish he asked to pray for his soul: his name is given to a square, place, street and road, and his charity still benefits churches in Islington. In the east window of Holy Trinity church the rich purple figure of Richard Cloudesley is part of the glass by Willement; and his vault is still tended in St Mary's churchyard. Holy Trinity, in outline remarkably like King's College chapel, Cambridge, seems to fill Cloudesley Square, but as Christopher Hussey pointed out, the church is effective from diagonal views but provides no central feature on the main, north–south axis. The church, one of the four designed by Charles Barry in Islington, no longer has galleries cutting across the long arched side-windows; this brings a classical emphasis to the building, perpendicular in style.

LONSDALE SQUARE

Lonsdale Square to the north was built between 1838 and 1842 on the site of the Gosseyfield, left to the Drapers' Company by the daughter of a former clerk, John Walter, to support almshouses he had founded in the seventeenth century. The towering gables reminiscent of Tudor rooftops may have had their inspiration from this connection. At ground level the churchlike front doors and pretty quatrefoil fanlights above are Gothic in character. Richard Cromwell Carpenter (1812–1855), who designed the square, was a friend of Pugin and built churches elsewhere before his death at the age of forty-three. In the 1960s the Friends Neighbourhood House started its welfare work for the community from the square; and many houses are now the pride of owner-occupiers (one of them being Richard Rodney Bennett, the composer) since the Drapers' Company sold them all in 1954. Forming a classical endpiece to the northern opening of this square is the Drapers' Arms with its long arched windows set between pillars. This public house also forms a centre-piece of the northern terrace of Barnsbury Street, restored by Kenneth Pring for the Barnsbury Housing Association to provide flats and maisonettes. On the corner of Barnsbury Street is a round, turreted Victorian building where colourful wedding parties crowded the pavements when it was Islington's registry office until 1965. This was formerly the site of the parish workhouse (reached by 'Cut-throat Lane') where the rigid diet was only varied on Christmas Day with roast-beef and plum-pudding, on Easter Monday with pork, and on Whit Monday with veal.

CHURCH MISSIONARY COLLEGE

On the five and a half acres known as Cooke's Fields, Thomas Cubitt (who later built Belgravia) developed College Cross and Manchester Terrace facing Liverpool Road, between 1827 and 1837. Cubitt, as master-builder, erected two houses in the centre of the north-facing terrace (ironically hardly recognizable as his work nowadays) which set the pattern for the other builders in this development. He had laid out the roads and plots and insisted on approving the fleur-de-lys pattern used in the iron railings though he does not seem to have enforced uniformity! The Church Missionary College from which College Cross took its name stood on the site of Sutton Dwellings from 1825 to 1915. The students here learnt Latin, Greek and Hebrew, as well as 'the rudiments at least of the language of the particular country to which their exertions are to be devoted'. James Elmes, the architect, described the building as 'a building more remarkable for its strength and goodness of construction than for elegance of design'. At the time of the Napoleonic wars the short-lived Loyal Islington Volunteer cavalry and infantry performed their exercises in fields in this neighbourhood. On the corner of Laycock Street and Liverpool Road stand the solid-brick Samuel Lewis buildings, where Mr Laycock, one of the richest dairy-farmers of his day, had his cattle pens. Unlike many other workmen's dwellings in Islington, these blocks interspaced by trees have a finish as good as any of their contemporary Kensington counterparts.

BARNSBURY PARK

The stucco peels from villas on the south side of Barnsbury Park; on the north side three have been turned into a petrol station, schoolhouse and timber warehouse. In 1827 these were the delight of a poet, who wrote this lighthearted suburban sonnet in Hone's Table Book:

> *You who are anxious for a country seat*
> *Pure air, green meadows and suburban views;*
> *Rooms snug and light – not overlarge but neat,*
> *And gardens water'd with refreshing dews,*
> *May find a spot adapted to your taste,*
> *Near Barnsbury Park, or rather Barnsbury Town*
> *Where everything looks elegant and chaste,*
> *And Wealth reposes on a bed of down.*

In the 1820s the Reverend Daniel Wilson, Vicar of St Mary's, founded the Islington Clerical Conference in his vicarage in

Barnsbury Park. Walter Sickert lived here in the 1930s with his third wife, Thérèse Lessore – and used the nearby Pentonville Prison as a landmark for directing the taxis he loved to use!

BARNSBURY SQUARE

In Barnsbury Square no side is the same as another: the east side is the former Minerva Terrace of the 1830s, facing Thornhill Road; on the south side is the bow-fronted West Lodge, now restored; to the west are Mountfort Terrace and Mountfort Crescent, with Mountfort House in the centre built in the 1840s as elegant as the Nash houses in Regent's Park; and on the north side postwar warders' houses adjoin an isolated pair of stately villas.

The lie of the land on the south and west sides suggests ram-

Belitha Villas

parts which might form a natural site for a Roman camp. Traditionally Suetonius Paulinus, the Roman governor of Britain, had his camp here before defeating Boadicea at Battle Bridge (now King's Cross) in A.D. 61. There is some support for this tradition since arrowheads were found here in 1825; and the stone sign of the twentieth legion was dug up by a labourer in 1842 north of Mountfort House. And the name Mountfort recalls these Roman associations.

In Mountfort House, formerly an elegant centre-piece of the west side but now a factory, Sir Johnston Forbes-Robertson (1853–1937), the best Hamlet of his day, first played the part to his sister's Ophelia in the drawing room in 1865. His father, John Forbes Robertson, was an art critic whose friends included William Morris, Arnold Bennett and Rossetti.

North of Barnsbury Square looms the large, grandiose fronts of the Victorian Belitha Villas – named after a lessee of the Angel – and the porticoed doors and steps, set well back from the road, display a touch of grandeur.

The Old Angel Inn by F. N. Shepherd

THOMAS ALBION OLDFIELD

Thornhill Road runs south past a gabled Victorian school, still with its schoolkeeper's entrance, to a village row of shops and the Albion public house with wisteria round its windows. The Albion flourished as a tea-garden in the early 1800s, catering for early cricketers, who played on the fields to the west until the summer of 1834 when the Albion Club moved to Copenhagen Fields. Thomas Albion Oldfield ran a dairy here; it was he who built the tea-house which eventually became a tavern. The pretty 1830s cottages of Albion Grove were renamed Ripplevale Grove in 1921 to honour Sir John French, later Earl of Ypres of Ripple Vale. The almost 'sea-side' cottages of Malvern Terrace front

Ripplevale Grove

Thornhill Square

on to the green of Thornhill Gardens, and not the promenade one would expect!

MR THORNHILL'S ESTATE

Building on Mr George Thornhill's estate of some eighty-six acres began in about 1820, though he had made earlier attempts to improve it since he thought it 'a property full of resources for great improvement'. The Chalk Road (later Caledonian Road) and Richmond Road, built in the 1820s, stimulated development. Among the first houses were those on the south-eastern side of Hemingford Road, which fetched £450 on a ninety-nine-year lease when the brick carcase was completed '. . . with fixtures, water closets, cupboards, stoves and every other thing required for the completion of the aforesaid home and premises. The three parlours and passage to be grained satin wood and wainscot'. The early residents of Hemingford Terrace soon complained of 'the shooting through the windows of some of the houses' and

Richmond Avenue

William Dennis, the builder, gave the local inspector 'full liberty to take into custody all parties trespassing upon our Ground'. It was not until 1844 that Dennis built the southern terrace in Richmond Avenue with sphinxes, as fierce as any hunting dog, guarding the doorsteps. While building these, he had to stop Mr Smith, the nurseryman, taking away 'great quantities of sand from the ground in front of Richmond Terrace' which left holes he had to fill with clay!

THORNHILL SQUARE

In the elliptical Thornhill Square, built in the 1850s, the large St Andrew's church (designed by Francis B. Newman and John Johnson) was built on a site given by George Thornhill. The *Ecclesiologist* thought the church 'an ostentatious cruciform pile, all gables and transepts, with an exaggerated broach'. The uniform sweep of the classical terraces is broken by the Edwardian west branch library designed in 1906 by Professor A. Beresford Pite, architect of the south end of Burlington Arcade.

CALEDONIAN ROAD

Until 1903, when the Royal Caledonian Asylum moved from the Caledonian Road, the orphans in jackets and kilts of the royal tartan brought a breath of Scotland to the neighbourhood. The orphanage opened in 1828 in isolated splendour as a monument to Scottish thrift, benefiting the children of soldiers and sailors. Samuel Lewis described the building as 'a spacious and handsome building of Suffolk brick, ornamented with freestone, with a boldly-projecting portico of four fluted columns of the Doric order, supporting a triangular pediment, in the tympanum of which is a shield bearing the arms of Scotland, and, on the apex, a full-length figure of St Andrew bearing his cross'. Between 1864 and 1888 the Great Northern Hospital was in the 'Cally', as the road is affectionately known, near to the site of the red-brick Caledonian Road baths. The hospital was founded in 1856 to serve the poor without letters of recommendation or other forms of admission, and moved to the Caledonian Road hoping for 'liberal support . . . by the rich inhabitants of the northern suburbs'. Dr Robert Bridges, later to become Poet Laureate, worked here as physician after showing his skill in dealing with a smallpox outbreak in 1876. The hospital moved to Holloway in 1888 and eventually became the Royal Northern Hospital.

PAGET'S MEMORIAL HALL

Between 1887 and 1889 Violet Mary Paget, daughter of Lord Alfred Paget and a deaconess of Mildmay, held Bible classes as part of the mission work in the neighbourhood. After her death, the Reverend Sholto Douglas Campbell, sometime Rector of All Souls, Langham Place, built a memorial hall on the spot at Randell's Road – a bizarre place with richly carved figures of Virtue and Vice. The breakfast set that Queen Victoria gave the couple is still kept here.

ST JAMES'S, PENTONVILLE

Henry Penton, Member of Parliament for Winchester where he lived, had some difficulty in building the chapel for his estate of Pentonville since the Vicar of Clerkenwell insisted on a bond for the minister's stipend. For the first four years St James's, Pentonville Road, was technically a dissenting chapel before being consecrated in 1791 as a chapel of ease to Clerkenwell parish church. Peter Ibbetson, in George du Maurier's novel of that name published in 1891, was apprenticed to Mr Lintot, architect and surveyor, and lodged near him in Pentonville. He 'disliked Pentonville, which, although clean, virtuous, and respectable, left much to be desired on the score of shape, colour, romantic tradition, and local charm'. The Lintots belonged to an old Pentonville family who gave exclusive parties! Mrs Lintot and her severely dressed friends would play 'Bach, or Hummel, or Scarlatti, each of whom, they would say, could write both like an artist and a gentleman – a very rare but indispensable combination, it seemed'.

WHITE CONDUIT TEA-GARDENS

The modern White Conduit public house in Barnsbury Road is on part of the site of the eighteenth-century tea-gardens Oliver Goldsmith frequented. Here Goldsmith one day met three daughters of a respectable tradesman to whom he owed some money. Washington Irving tells the story as follows: 'With his prompt disposition to oblige, he conducted them about the garden, treated them to a tea, and ran up a bill in the most open-hearted manner imaginable; it was only when he came to pay that he found himself in one of his old dilemmas – he had not the wherewithal in his pocket. A scene of perplexity now took place between him and the waiter, in the midst of which came up some of his acquaintances, in whose eyes he wished to stand particularly well. When, however, they had enjoyed their banter, the waiter was paid, and poor Goldsmith enabled to carry off the ladies with flying colours.'

Robert Bartholomew, the owner, added a long walk in 1754 to the gardens already laid out with a fish-pond and pleasant arbours. He also provided bats and balls for those who wished to play cricket in the adjoining meadow. Between 1780 and 1787 the gentlemen of the White Conduit Club played here, and the club was 'the acorn from which sprang the gigantic oak known as the M.C.C.' One of the members, the Earl of Winchelsea, suggested to Thomas Lord, who was in his service and bowled to members in practice, that if he made a private ground he would be well supported. By 1787 Lord's first ground was ready for use, and the M.C.C. was formed. In 1825 the White Conduit gardens were advertised as the 'new Vauxhall' and the Battle of Waterloo was commemorated with a grand gala and rural fête with a concert and fireworks. But in 1827 Hone described the evening's entertainment as 'a starveling show of odd company and coloured lamps, a mock orchestra with mock singing, dancing in a room which decent persons would prefer to withdraw their young folks from if they entered'. Five of the Tolpuddle martyrs were welcomed back from Australia here with a grand dinner of cold beef, ham, hot pies, and plum pudding; but by 1849 'Vite Cundick Couse', as Cockneys knew it, was demolished to make way for the public house.

On the site of the present Belvedere Tavern was Busby's Folly, a tea-garden which took its name in 1668 from Christopher Busbee, landlord of the nearby White Lion. Until the 1860s the Belvedere Tavern was well known for its bowling green and rackets court. Off Penton Street is Starcross School, a comprehensive girls' school which replaced the controversial Rising Hill co-educational comprehensive in 1966. The building, with its sunken playgrounds built from former basements, won a Civic Trust award in 1961.

THREE HATS AND DOBNEYS

Behind the Three Hats, which stood until 1839 near the turnpike gate in Islington High Street, Thomas Johnson, 'the Irish Tartar', rode on two, three and four horses in turn. Sampson, who performed similar equestrian feats there, was ensnared into 'gay company' by his rival Price at Dobneys, and eventually was forced to sell his horses to another performer! In the eighteenth century, Thomas Topham, 'the strong man of Islington', was the landlord of the Duke's Head in St Alban's Place. He showed his strength by lifting two hogsheads of water, heaving his horse over the turnpike gate, and rolling up a pewter dish (said to be in the British Museum) with his fingers. This muscular Samson was not without his Delilah – in 1749 he stabbed his unfaithful wife and then himself; he died but she survived.

Sir Walter Raleigh is said to have lived at the Old Pied Bull which was near the site of the modern public house on the corner of Theberton Street and Upper Street, though the coat of arms found in the old inn belonged to Sir John Miller! Near the King's Head opposite St Mary's church, Kate Greenaway's mother ran a children's clothes shop in the 1840s to support the family. Kate, who was to delight thousands with her illustrations of child-life, had her first drawing lessons in Canonbury.

VI

Highbury

HISTORY

LIKE the Canons of St Bartholomew, the Knights of St John of
Jerusalem had a country retreat in Islington: traditionally known
as Highbury Castle, theirs overlooked the hills of Highbury on
the site of Eton House, Leigh Road. This manor house had been
given to the Knights in 1271 by Alicia de Barowe together with
the manor; the house was built on higher ground than an existing
one in Tolentone, which was later referred to as the 'Lower Place'.
The manor, which embraced both Highbury and Tollington, was
consequently known as Highbury rather than Tolentone, and had
the additional name of Newington Barrow. This may have been
derived from Lady Alicia de Barowe, though she could just as
easily have taken the name from her estate.

In 1281 the priory of the Knights of St John of Jerusalem in
Finsbury was burnt down in the peasant revolt led by Wat Tyler.
A mob some 20,000 strong led by Jack Straw turned their fury
on Highbury Castle which they had some difficulty in destroying
as it was built of stone. Not surprisingly the spot then became
known as Jack Straw's castle. With the dissolution of the monasteries, the Knights lost the manor as well. This passed to Thomas
Cromwell, who held the manor, together with Canonbury, for a
short time only before being executed. The manor, which reverted
to the Crown until Charles I parted with it, was held between
1723 and 1791 by James Colebrooke, the largest landowner in
the parish of St Mary, and Sir George Colebrooke. In 1651 the
two woods, Highbury and Little St John's, passed into the
possession of Henry Mildmay, who had sat in judgement on
Charles I, and Richard Clutterbuck, who paid some £300 for the

forests covering the forty-three acres of Highbury Woods and the thirty-five acres of Little St John's Wood: 'From that time, the trees, appearing to have been immediately cut down, all traces have vanished of the ancient forest honours of Tolentone or Highbury.' The names the Victorian builders gave to their rows of mansions, such as 'Aberdeen Park', 'Hamilton Park' and 'Aubert Park' sound like country houses and evoke some nostalgia for these woods.

CHARACTER

The tree-lined walks and open green of Highbury Fields make up Islington's only large park. In the eighteenth century Oliver Goldsmith and his friends would walk through the fields to Highbury Barn for their dinner of two courses and pastry, for which they paid tenpence a head, including the waiter's penny! The remaining Highbury Fields are now surrounded by houses but provide an open space for the enjoyment of footballers, tennis players, walkers and children; and swimmers use an open-air pool. The grounds of Arsenal, Islington's football team, are to the north of Highbury Fields.

Had Victorian speculators not been so greedy, Highbury Fields might well have been part of a park as green and magnificent as any royal one, with the main entrance in Highbury Place. In 1850 Mr Lloyd mooted a park which, with its five hundred acres, would have been larger than Regent's Park or Hyde Park, stretching from Highbury to Green Lanes and from Stamford Hill to Holloway. Although he had enlisted the support of the Prince Consort, Lord Robert Grosvenor, Lord Ashley and Lord Carlisle, he failed in his attempt to raise the £200,000 necessary to secure the land. The fund raisers knew that unless the land was bought immediately it would be built over within a year, and they proved no match for the builders. If not within the year, at least within the decade, the fields were covered with the villas and park-like mansions which were show-pieces for Victorian affluence. Finsbury Park was opened to the north in 1869 as a consolation prize, mainly for those living in Finsbury. But the park of 120 acres, which cost £95,000, is not within the borough of Islington. For those living in Islington the consolation prize of Highbury Fields was somewhat smaller and came later: in

1885 the twenty-seven acres of this park were bought for £60,000 – half of which was paid by the vestry of Islington, the other half by the Metropolitan Board of Works.

Highbury and the adjoining Mildmay are bounded by Holloway Road to the west, St Paul's Road to the south, Stoke Newington to the east, and Seven Sisters Road to the north.

HIGHBURY HOUSE

From 1781 until 1938 Highbury House, built by John Dawes (who rebuilt part of Canonbury House), stood on the site of Eton House, Leigh Road; and some of the servants' wing may still be seen behind Christchurch Hall in Leigh Road. This 'elegant and commodious' house with its shrubberies, paddocks and hothouses covering some seventy-four acres cost Dawes £10,000 to erect. After his death in 1788 the house, which must have had a commanding view over Highbury Fields to the south, was bought by Alexander Aubert. He only paid 6,000 guineas for Highbury House, then hemmed in by two terraces, where he lived as a squire until his death in 1805. As Nelson commented: 'This gentleman was particularly endeared to the inhabitants of Islington for his good humour, hospitality, affability, and politeness towards them upon every occasion.' Aubert 'being a tory in principle' was from time to time associated with the most eminent members of that party amongst whom were Mr William Pitt and Mr Henry Dundas. He had the surrounding moat partially filled in to make a carriageway to the house and improved the gardens. Aubert was a Fellow of the Royal Society and a keen astronomer, though never as eminent as Edmund Halley who had also made lunar observations in Islington. At Highbury House he built a 'spacious and lofty observatory' with a rotary roof and equipped with apparatus envied by astronomers all over Europe.

The Loyal Islington Volunteers

In 1797 Alexander Aubert became Lieutenant-Colonel commanding the infantry of the Loyal Islington Volunteers. It was formed at his initiative to help prevent the spread of the French Revolution. When the corps of more than 300 members received its colours, Aubert gave an open-air dinner-dance at Highbury

House to which 'nearly all the respectable inhabitants of Islington were invited'. So proud was Alexander Aubert of his position that he had a full-length portrait painted of himself with the corps in the background drawn up in military array; he himself stood, holding his charger, in the splendid uniform of a blue jacket with scarlet and silver lace trimmings, and white kerseymere pantaloons. The only active service the Volunteers saw before they were disbanded in 1801 was a march under arms to a large meeting of the London Corresponding Society in the fields near Copenhagen House; but before they arrived the City Light Horse had dispersed the crowds! The Volunteers reformed in 1803 for three years; but under a different command, with a different uniform, and drilled by an army adjutant, they 'soon arrived to great perfection in order and discipline'. The shrubberies where the Volunteers danced to quadrille bands was swept away to form the promenade of huge stout villas on Highbury Hill, still standing with the dignity of dowager-duchesses.

HIGHBURY PLACE

The first terraces built in Highbury were those in Highbury Place dating from the 1770s, and Highbury Terrace dating from the 1780s, which stood for some time alone. Their views over Highbury Fields are still open ones but the far-reaching outlook they had eastwards to 'Limehouse church, Greenwich Hospital and park, and the vessels navigating the river Thames' is gone. Nelson thought the thirty-nine houses which form Highbury Place 'one of the finest rows of houses in the environs of the Metropolis'. These were built for City merchants by John Spiller who himself lived in No. 39, now the area office of the Electrical Trade Union. The originality of this terrace, marred by later distortions, may still be traced in the unusual way in which some of the door pediments are designed. A few iron lamp-holders bridging the entrance gaps in the iron railings indicate how necessary some form of street lighting was in the private road in front, 'frequented only by the carriages passing to and fro, from the several dwellings between the village and Highbury House'. These houses were equipped with coach houses for the owners' carriages; they were 'mostly on a large scale, with good gardens behind, and allotments of meadow-land across the road in front'.

Abraham Newland

Mr Spiller, however, had to wait some time for a return on his speculation: for in 1835 the historian Cromwell related that many of the houses remained unoccupied at first and others were let at very low rents. 'For many years past, however, these residences have been considered, in every point of view, so desirable, as to command thrice the sums for which they were let to the original inhabitants.' Among those who first moved in was Abraham Newland, Chief Cashier of the Bank of England, who 'lived' at Highbury Place until his death in 1807. Newland's name had a circulation throughout the country on the bank notes on which his signature appeared, which led Charles Dibdin, manager of Sadler's Wells, to write these lines:

> *The world is inclined to think Justice is blind,*
> *But lawyers know well she can view land;*
> *But, lor, what of that – she'll blink like a bat*
> *At the sight of an 'Abraham Newland'.*

Whether Newland 'lived' at Highbury Place is debatable since he slept every night at the Bank of England and only spent two months of his retirement in Highbury. Coull says that Newland would go to his house after dining in his rooms at the Bank, drink tea with his housekeeper, walk in the garden or the gravel way to Highbury Barn and then return to the Bank. He devoted the same scrutiny to his household expenses as he would to any bank account; 'before the close of the day the domestic transactions were entered in a book, cast up and checked, so that, to a farthing, the rich man might see that the outlay and receipts balanced correctly.' No wonder that he left a fortune of some £130,000.

John Nichols

John Nichols, editor of the *Gentleman's Magazine* for nearly fifty years, lived in Highbury Place; his son and grandson were to carry on the magazine after Nichols's death in 1826. Nichols, who was born opposite the parish church and buried there, was an outstanding publisher of topographical works. In 1763 he wrote a poem about Islington and in 1788 wrote the first work about the area, *A History of Canonbury*. From 1780 to 1790 with the help of Richard Gough he brought out the *Bibliotheca Topographica Britannica*, a collection of rare topographical manuscripts; and among other works he was the publisher of *The History of the County of Leicester*.

Joseph Chamberlain

In the 1840s Joseph Chamberlain, the statesman, spent his boyhood at No. 25 Highbury Place (as a plaque denotes): the large house was, as his biographer J. L. Garvin relates, 'a lovable home; long afterwards Chamberlain remembered it acutely when he came to his saddest hours'. Here the young Chamberlain at the age of nine spoke as a Unitarian minister from a pulpit formed by the high board back of a large chair, covered in white dimity; at the age of eighteen he went to Birmingham to make his fortune and his mark as a politician – and called his home there 'Highbury'.

Sickert's Studio

In a ground-floor room of No. 1 Highbury Place (as a plaque denotes) Sickert, the painter greatly influenced by Degas, ran a school of painting and a studio, between 1927 and 1934. The school was for male students only and with no models; among the students were Mark Oliver, Lord Methuen, Morland Lewis and Dr Robert Emmons (later Sickert's biographer). 'Most of the time', Dr Emmons relates, 'we sat in a semi-circle round the fire and listened to the professor talk. It went on for hours. But it was never too much. When everything had been said, we were allowed to work. . . . Sickert came in every morning in a different hat. After going the rounds, he settled down by the fire with a Manilla and the whole of the Metropolitan press. Little by little he came less often. The students drifted away. The school came to an end by a process of evaporation.' At this studio, Sickert finished the full-length portrait of Rear-Admiral Lumsden rejected by the Royal Academy in 1927 but accepted the following year. He started the 'Raising of Lazarus' by painting the first design directly on to the red wallpaper which lined the room; he painted the portraits of Winston Churchill, Sir Hugh Walpole and Sir Nigel Playfair here and also 'Lazarus breaks his Fast' and the pictures of Barnet Fair.

HIGHBURY TERRACE

Shortly after Highbury Terrace was built, one of the sisters of Samuel Rogers, the banker-poet, described it as 'quite a gay place,

Print of Highbury Terrace, *c.* 1837

more like the seaside than anything else'. After Samuel Rogers had sold their family house in Stoke Newington, his brother Henry and another sister came to live in the terrace. To the north were two detached mansions, 'Highbury Lodge' and 'Highbury Hill'. The terrace itself, with slender main-floor windows and iron balconies, is much the same as when first built; like vintage wine, it has matured well. Mr Charles Wheelwright, who commanded the re-formed Loyal Islington Volunteers, lived in Highbury Terrace, within a stone's throw of Alexander Aubert's Highbury

House at the top of the hill. So did Captain Joseph Huddart, an Elder Brother of Trinity House, whose maps and charts made him one of the great geographers of his day. One of these houses has been carefully restored by Julian and Renée Robinson, the fashion designers, whose huge basement-kitchen with its collection of early kitchen utensils has been featured in many magazines and books. The south-western side of Highbury Fields sweeps round in a crescent of 1840s villas in pairs, to the southern tip where a war memorial, erected after the Boer War and designed by Bertram McKennal R.A., has pride of place. During the Second World War more than a score were killed and many more injured by a flying bomb at Highbury Corner – ironically near the Angel of Peace.

CHRISTCHURCH

At the north-eastern side of Highbury Fields stands the ragstone Christchurch of 1848, in design much more an artist's than an architect's church. As the *Illustrated London News* commented at the time on Thomas Allom's plan: 'From whatever point it is viewed, the building presents a varied and striking form.' The church is surrounded by flowers without a trace of a churchyard on a site given by Henry Dawes, honouring the original building committee's demands that the 'building must not be unsightly, nor the ground used for burials'. The exterior of the church gives the impression of a huddle of small chapels; but the interior with its slender arches forming a delicate Gothic roof does not bear this out. The windows by Francis Spear, which were part of the postwar restoration, were made by a local glassmaker. Near the church is an ornate clock tower marking Queen Victoria's Diamond Jubilee.

HIGHBURY NEW PARK

The palazzo-like villas of Highbury New Park have a strange *Dolce Vita* feeling with their neglected fronts, ragged balustraded walls and ill-kept gardens. These once formed a 'stockbroker belt' against which some Victorian ministers would rail. Charles Booth, in his survey of the London poor, commented that the majority of the inhabitants here belonged to the wealthy class with coachmen living in the mews. The carriageways are silent now: the coach houses no longer have their victorias; and the stucco, cracked and peeling, cries out for a face-lift in places. The huge St Augustine church now has a church hall crammed in its interior where the Victorian paterfamilias and his household once filled the pews. The site of the Athenaeum is built over with council housing and from the 1930s to the 1960s there were film studios here. After the Second World War, Rank bought the studios and, with John Croydon as producer, used them to make second features, training young directors, actors and technicians. Among them was Terence Fisher, who directed *To the Public Danger* here with Susan Shaw (Patsy Sloots, the daughter of a Dutch band-leader) in the lead. Here also Rank opened a charm school to give a Hollywood grooming to promising young actresses under Miss Molly Terraine; Diana Dors was one of her young pupils.

ABERDEEN PARK

The private estate of Aberdeen Park emphasizes its exclusiveness by a no-entry sign barring all but residents and their callers! The park, built when Lord Aberdeen was at the peak of his political career, now contains houses representing many different eras from early Victorian to suburban-semi, and the few original houses which Sir John Betjeman described as 'solid Italianate houses for the solid commercial mind' languish for lack of money and minions.

Here Betjeman's parents knew:

> *The brougham that crunched the gravel, the laurel-girt*
> *paths that wind,*
> *Geranium-beds for the lawn, Venetian blinds for the sun,*
> *A separate trademan's entrance, straw in the mews behind,*
> *Just in the four-mile radius where hackney carriages run.*

On Sundays the residents of Aberdeen Park crowded into St Saviour's, now shrouded in gloom and hidden by spawning green undergrowth. Inside, the dull red brick is decorated in parts with blue and cream patterns. This almost medieval-looking church was built in 1865 despite protests from the Reverend Daniel Wilson that the offer to do so came from 'one identified with the

Romanizing movement in our Church'. Clarke considers the church one of the best designed by William White, and Betjeman remembers the church as

Great red church of my parents, cruciform crossing they knew –
Over these same encaustics they and their parents trod
Bound through a brick-red transept for a once familiar pew
Where the organ set them singing and the sermon let them nod.

In Highbury Grove near the site of a Victorian truant school, a comprehensive designed by James Cubitt opened in 1967. Highbury Grove comprehensive is run by the present headmaster, Dr Rhodes Boyson, a well-known educationist, on the 'house' method usually associated with public schools. The buildings, which cost £665,000, include a swimming bath, gymnasium, art and music rooms, a forge, engineering and work rooms, science laboratories, and a floodlit football pitch.

HIGHBURY BARN

In the modern public house of Highbury Barn in Highbury Park is a painting of the pleasure gardens which made the spot so popular in the eighteenth and nineteenth centuries. This shows the Leviathan open-air dancing platform built in the 1850s, set in gardens where the avenues were lit by gas lamps held by female statues. Edward Giovanelli added a spacious ball and supper room in the 1860s where Leotard, the gymnast, performed. He built the Alexandra theatre in the grounds and Blondin, the tight-rope walker, Natator, the man-frog, and the Siamese Twins were billed. Giovanelli's neighbours were so disturbed by the riotous behaviour of the dancers and theatre-goers that in 1870 he lost his dancing licence and the following year Highbury Barn was closed. The days of 'monster dinner-parties' in the Great Room formed from the barn of Highbury Grange (or farm) had gone long before: in 1841, for instance, three thousand sat down to the Licensed Victuallers' Dinner. As Wroth writes: 'The flower-beds became choked with grass and weeds, and nightshade luxuriated around the dismantled orchestra'; by 1883 the gardens were built over.

EARLY VILLAS

Close to Highbury Barn is a fine Regency terrace, set back from the road with delicate ironwork and frieze, confusingly known as Park Terrace! Nearly opposite this Thomas Cubitt, builder of the east wing of Buckingham Palace, built 'a row of genteel and commodious villas' in the 1820s. The two most northerly ones (Nos. 54 and 56 Highbury Park) remain, but those nearer Highbury Barn were probably more elegant as they formed the pattern for other bow-fronted houses in Highbury Grange. Aubert Park, a mixture of bow-fronted cottages and grand villas, takes its name from Alexander Aubert who lived at Highbury House; at No. 17 the eagles on the gatepost seem appropriate, for this is the former home of Sir Arthur Keith, the Scottish anthropologist, known for his work on anthropoid apes and ancient man. The modern Catholic church of St Joan of Arc in Highbury Park dates from the 1960s; it was built at a cost of £82,000 to a design by Stanley C. Kerr Bates. Since 1925 the headquarters of the

A Villa in Highbury New Park

National Children's Home has been in Highbury Park. The organization was founded by Dr Thomas Bowman Stephenson, a Wesleyan minister, in 1869. Like Dr Barnardo, Stephenson was a pioneer in establishing children's homes throughout the country for orphans and displaced children who he thought should live in a family-like atmosphere.

HIGHBURY COLLEGE AND ARSENAL

Until 1913 the Highbury theological college stood on the site of Arsenal – which meant that for a time no football could be played on religious holidays there. The college, founded at Mile End in 1783 as a Congregationalist training institution, moved to Highbury in 1826 to a building forming 'three sides of a parallelogram, and [with] a beautiful view from its garden or back front, towards Highgate, Hampstead, Hornsey . . .' The forty or so men who studied here had to have the minimum entrance qualifications of 'such preparatory education in Latin as will enable them to read

Virgil, and with some knowledge of fractional arithmetic and the elements of geography: their piety, and ministerial talents, must be attested by the pastor and church to which they belong, or by some other evidence satisfactory to the Committee'.

In 1913 the Arsenal footballers in their red shirts took over the six acres of Highbury College, moving from Woolwich where munition workers had formed the club in 1886. Their move was not without opposition: their neighbours complained that it would upset the peace of 'a quiet backwater of London', and Tottenham Hotspur thought there were not enough supporters for two professional clubs in north London. During the First World War the two rival clubs shared Highbury Stadium; and during the Second World War they shared White Hart Lane.

Highbury Stadium. Arsenal *v.* Sheffield United taking advantage of the underground heating in the winter of 1968

'*The Double*'

The story of Arsenal's triumphs and defeats has been told many times. Their struggles have become legendary after they became the second team this century to 'win the Double' – a decade after Spurs, their arch-rivals. In the 1970–71 season they beat Spurs 1–0 in the final match of their League season at White Hart Lane to become League champions and overcame Liverpool 2–1 after extra time in the Cup Final at Wembley the same week. After the First World War, Arsenal won their First Division place by ballot when the division was enlarged – polling eighteen votes to Spurs's eight; they were fortuituously promoted while Spurs were relegated and some say this is the origin of their 'Lucky Arsenal' tag. The team won their first F.A. Cup victory in 1929–30 when they beat Huddersfield Town. During the 1930s Arsenal were League champions five times over, and the England selectors once picked seven players from the club for an international match against Italy. No wonder then that Gillespie Road underground station was renamed Arsenal!

THE CENTRAL PUBLIC LIBRARY

The ratepayers in Islington had long thought public libraries an extravagance and for some thirty years opposed the adoption of the Public Libraries Act. Finally, in 1907, the central public library was opened in Holloway Road with a ball, the corridors and stairs being carpeted and decorated with flowers and ferns. The recently established borough council had finally adopted the Act, and Andrew Carnegie, the Scottish multi-millionaire, had made their duty less painful by donating £40,000 towards the building of the central library and four branch libraries. The building, with its statues of Bacon and Spenser in the front, was designed by Henry Hare, architect of Oxford and Henley town halls. Apart from an extensive local collection this library also has a valuable Sickert collection. The red-brick building of the former Northern Polytechnic in Holloway Road (now part of the Polytechnic of North London) is linked to a tower-block of the 1960s by a concrete mural by William Mitchell.

MILDMAY

The district of Mildmay to the east of Highbury takes its name from one of the judges of Charles I, Sir Henry Mildmay, who held land there in the seventeenth century. He had married the daughter of Alderman Halliday whose mansion on the south side of Newington Green stood in more than forty acres of pasture. When Charles II was restored to the throne, Mildmay lost all his estates apart from Stoke Newington, which had been settled on his wife. Coull suggests that Mildmay's brother Anthony may have intervened; ironically while Mildmay had judged Charles I, Anthony had shown his devotion to the King to the last.

NEWINGTON GREEN

The Bishop's Palace, with its richly gilded wainscoting, stood to the north-east of Newington Green until 1800; traditionally this was one of Henry VIII's hunting lodges, and Henry's Walk is said to run along a path he used. There is some evidence that Henry Percy, Earl of Northumberland, stayed at Newington Green, for he wrote a letter from there to the King denying that he had married Anne Boleyn; and on his death the next year he left most of his estates to the King. Three sides of Newington Green belong to Islington; only the north of the Green is within Stoke Newington itself. In 1861 Coull commented that 'perhaps there is no single spot in the district where there are so many quaint, but commodious, old-fashioned red-brick mansions as those situated round the enclosure mentioned'. But only a few of these houses remain on the west side – one with the date 1658 indicating its Jacobean past.

NONCONFORMISTS

The Green was popular with nonconformists towards the end of the seventeenth century; among these were Luke Milbourn, Charles Morton (at whose school Daniel Defoe, author of *Robinson Crusoe*, was educated for four years), the Reverend M. Starkey and Jonathan Screw. In 1746 Dr Samuel Wright died leaving some £20,000 to charity; he wrote in one of his books:

'I had rather be the author of a small book that shall be instrumental in saving a soul from sin and death, than of the finest piece of science and literature in the world that leads only to accomplishments for the present state of being.' At Newington Green, Mary Wollstonecraft, the Anglo-Irish feminist, met Samuel Johnson and came under the influence of Dr Richard Price, the brilliant nonconformist divine. She and her sister Eliza kept a school from 1783 to 1787 in this neighbourhood.

Stoke Newington House, the home of Samuel Rogers, the banker-poet, is said to have stood on the corner of Ferntower and Newington Green roads. On the north side of Ball's Pond Road, forming a Tudor-style courtyard, are the Metropolitan Benefit Society's almshouses, built in 1836. One of the gateposts records that Mary Ann Mackenzie, who died in 1881, gave nearly £9,000 to the almshouses.

VII

Holloway

HOLLOWAY ROAD, which runs from Highbury Corner to the foot of Highgate Hill, was traditionally once a *hollow way* filled in with gravel by a hermit to make a causeway for travellers to and from the north. This hermit took the gravel from the top of Highgate Hill where he lived to form a much-needed pond there, thus 'providing water on the hill, where it was wanting, and cleanness in the valley, which before, especially in winter was passed with great difficulty'. In 1473 William Pole, a leper himself, was granted land at the foot of Highgate Hill for a leper hospital near the Whittington stone.

The stone, which marks the spot where Dick Whittington is said to have heard the sound of Bow Bells in the 1370s, seems to have been connected originally with a wayside cross near the leper hospital.

During the coaching days of the seventeenth and eighteenth centuries, the road was lined with terraces and wayside inns, some of which remain to this day, such as the Mother Red Cap and the Half Moon. The latter was famed for the delicacy of its cheese-cakes in the eighteenth century: these were touted through the London streets by men on horseback. Country lanes led to tea-gardens such as Copenhagen House or those off Hornsey Lane, part of which was known as Duval's Lane. This was said to be the haunt of Claude Du Val, the handsome highwayman, who was executed at Tyburn in 1669 at the age of twenty-six. After his body had 'lain in state' at a tavern, 'he was buried in the middle aisle of Covent Garden church; and his funeral was attended with many flambeaux, and a numerous train of mourners, whereof most were of the beautiful sex'.

The fashionable suburb of Pentonville, which gave its name to the model prison in the new Caledonian Road which led from it, has disappeared. When a second prison was built in the 1850s the authorities masked it with the fortress-front of Warwick Castle as a sop to Victorian sensibilities. In time the City House of Correction, as this prison was known, became 'Holloway', London's prison for women; and now the front is to disappear when the prison is rebuilt to provide offenders with the hospital-like care that contemporary sensibilities demand. At Ring Cross, situated at the corner of Liverpool Road and Holloway Road, criminals were publicly executed at gallows 'a little beyond the two-mile stone'. In 1712 William Johnson was hanged at Holloway for shooting the turnkey of Newgate in open court at the Old Bailey.

CHARACTER

Holloway Road nowadays is a wide shopping thoroughfare and part of the A.1 route to the north. The late Victorian suburbs with their trim bow-fronted 'semis' and terraces stretch to the north of the borough where John Nash designed the original stone Highgate Archway. This was replaced by the present steel bridge by Sir Alexander Binnie at the end of the nineteenth century. The Whittington complex of amalgamated hospitals lies at the foot of Highgate Hill while the Royal Northern Hospital transferred to its present site in Holloway Road towards the end of the nineteenth century.

Some of the villas on the Tufnell estate, owned by the Lords of the Manor of Barnsbury, were designed by George Truefitt who was surveyor to the estate and lived at 1 Middleton Grove in the 1860s, and later at 'Fernbank', Carleton Road. The brash individuality is most marked in part of Anson Road where every villa is different. At Tollington Park whole blocks are different. The Georgian concept of houses as units of a well-proportioned terrace has no place in the district of Tollington Park; this was laid out in the 1860s by Gough and Roumieu mainly in Italianate style.

Holloway is not without its fun: Edward Lear, who wrote the *Book of Nonsense* for the Earl of Derby's grandchildren in 1846, was born there in 1812. He spent his childhood at Bowman's

Lodge, which took its name from an Elizabethan archery house and was on the site of Bowman's Mews.

George and Weedon Grossmith set their fictional *The Diary of a Nobody* in Holloway. Charles and Carrie Pooter 'moved' into the Holloway the Victorians thought so desirable and respectable; their house, 'The Laurels', Brickfield Terrace, was a six-roomed residence, excluding the basement, with a front breakfast-parlour where they could see and be seen by passers-by. In *The Diary of a Nobody* Mr Pooter, a City clerk, recounts his disputes with the tradesmen – the grocer's boy picks off the paint blisters on the side door; his do-it-yourself ventures such as painting the bath red since it was the 'best colour'; and his sallies into society, meeting characters such as Mr Murray Posh who claimed to take 'no active part' in business.

Upper and Lower Holloway are bounded by Hornsey Lane to the north, Stroud Green Road to the east, Seven Sisters Road–Holloway Road–Broad Street line to the south, and York Way and Dartmouth Park Hill to the west.

CALEDONIAN CATTLE MARKET

The thirty acres of the 'Cally' which made this former cattle market five times as large as the one in Smithfield it replaced, are now a mixture of green open space and red council housing. In Market Road some of the cast-iron railings with their bulls' heads which formed the boundary of this colossal trading ground remain. Under the large clock tower – still a landmark for miles around – farmers and butchers met to deal in thousands of cattle, sheep, calves and pigs in the sale room, with the banks and telegraph office conveniently nearby. Of the public houses they used, situated at the corners of the market, three still stand, somewhat isolated now: the Lamb, the Lion and the Horse (later White Horse); the Black Bull has been demolished.

On 13 June 1855 the Prince Consort opened the new market designed by J. B. Bunning, the architect of Holloway Prison; more than three million blue Staffordshire bricks and granite paving throughout gave this meat market of London a permanency which could never be disturbed, or so the Victorians thought. The drovers and traders no longer crowded into the congested Smithfield; the new market was served by two main roads and two separate railway systems, and unlike an earlier market built by John Perkins, the 'Cally' was to remain in use until 1963, though for the last part of its existence it was a wholesale meat market only. The petition to the Commons by the neighbouring residents had not prevented the enabling Act, backed by the Corporation of London, from being passed; the residents had protested since 'the bustle, confusion and inconvenience of an objectionable traffic from its present legitimate and accustomed locality to the neighbourhood of Islington' would affect their property and amenities. The Corporation had bought the seventy-five acres of Copenhagen Fields and built the market at a cost of more than £350,000.

COPENHAGEN HOUSE

Since the seventeenth century Copenhagen House, set in the open country, was a popular resort for Londoners; it stood on the site of the Caledonian market. Samuel Lewis comments that 'no

Copenhagen House

F.

house of the kind commands so extensive and uninterrupted a view of the metropolis and the immense western suburb, with the heights of Hampstead and Highgate, and the rich intervening meadows.' While Mrs Harrington ran Copenhagen House in the late eighteenth century, fives, skittles and Dutch-pins were part of the entertainment; and after she was brutally robbed in 1780 so many visitors came that a new extension was built. The meetings of the London Corresponding Society in Copenhagen Fields during the French Revolution caused some alarm, and on one occasion the City Light Horse dispersed a meeting. In the early nineteenth century the sport of bull-baiting and fights between bull-dogs in front of the house got so out of hand that the land-lord Tooth lost his licence. The house became a tea-garden which was especially popular during hay harvests in the surrounding fields. In 1834 the Metropolitan trade unions met on the privately owned fields, at the start of their protest march against the sentences imposed on the Tolpuddle martyrs for administering illegal oaths; two years later free pardons were given to the six farm labourers from Dorset. Nowadays the name lingers on in Copenhagen Street, in Barnsbury. Traditionally a Danish prince or ambassador is said to have lived at Copenhagen House during the time of the Plague, though another account has it that the house was opened by a Dane when the King of Denmark came to visit his brother-in-law James I in 1606.

CALEDONIAN 'FLEA MARKET'

On Fridays (and for a time Tuesdays) the Caledonian market was London's biggest 'flea market' until the outbreak of the Second World War; now the pedlars' market, first part of St Bartholomew's Fair at Smithfield, has moved to Bermondsey. Whole attics of junk were spread on the stones of the Caledonian market where thousands of buyers scavenged for their particular 'dreamfind' and then did some oriental bargaining with dealers who knew they were selling legends – at a price. J. B. Priestley, in *Self-Selected Essays* (1932), recounts how American tourists would pay over the odds for a silver bowl or an amber necklace, for the story of how they picked these up would probably be worth a lot more when they returned. H. V. Morton, when he visited the market in the 1920s, was

'deeply touched to think that any living person could need many
of the things displayed for sale. For all around me, lying on
sacking, were the driftwood and wreckage of a thousand lives:
door knobs, perambulators *in extremis*, bicycle wheels, bell
wire, bed knobs, old clothes, awful pictures, broken mirrors,
unromantic china goods, gaping false teeth, screws, nuts, bolts,
and vague pieces of rusty iron, whose mission in life, or whose
part and portion of a whole, Time had obliterated . . .

As I walked between the aisles of junk I remembered the
story of a friend who went to this market out of curiosity, and
came away unexpectedly in a taxicab with a priestess. He had
bought a mummy for ten shillings. And well can I believe it.
I longed for something like this to happen to me, for that is
how life should go.'

No wonder then that Walter Sickert is said to have thought
the Caledonian market his idea of heaven!

PENTONVILLE MODEL PRISON

The model prison of Pentonville was nearly built in Camden
Town, but Sir Joshua Jebb, the architect and first Surveyor
General of Prisons, thought the site too steep; so he was happy to
accept Thomas Cubitt's offer of a more level site in the new
Chalk Road (later Caledonian) which led from the bottom of
Pentonville hill. Behind the high perimeter walls some barred
windows set in brick are all that are visible to the outside world
of Jebb's radial building; this was modelled on Haviland's
Eastern Penitentiary at Philadelphia. The main entrance, with its
green studded doors and portcullis work in the archway, fronts
on to a slip road separated from the Caledonian Road by a
curtain wall; according to Henry Mayhew this was designed by
Sir Charles Barry.

The Separate System

Pentonville is a medium-security prison nowadays where mainly
short-term prisoners – such as the five dockers held in contempt
of court in 1972 – are committed. When it was built in 1842 at
a cost of more than £85,000, this 'model' prison provoked much

comment and debate. Though the horrors of overcrowding were avoided then, the separate system which kept prisoners apart from each other to prevent 'contamination' seemed a worse evil. The prisoners were confined to their cells and had limited contact with officers and instructors. They attended chapel in separate cubicles, and exercised at first in separate pens, later some twenty paces apart on concentric paths. They wore masks to prevent recognition by other prisoners and their activities took place in silence. Though the system led to lunacy in certain cases, the separate system was to influence the development of prisons throughout the rest of the country during the nineteenth century.

Charles Dickens felt so strongly that the system was wrong that he satirized it in his novel, *David Copperfield*, in 1850: The prison was 'an immense and solid building, erected at vast expense' in which the prisoners were addressed by numbers in order to protect their identities. David Copperfield who found Uriah Heep there, questions the advantages of the system, and finds them to be 'the perfect isolation of prisoners so that no one man in confinement there knew anything about another; and the

Exercise in the prison yard

reduction of prisoners to a wholesome state of mind, leading to sincere contrition and repentance'. Others were more than convinced that Pentonville was a model prison: Jane Welsh Carlyle, a doctor's daughter who visited the prison with her husband Thomas Carlyle, wrote to an uncle in Liverpool in 1851:

> I am sure, however, you would be amused with an account of our visit the other day to Pentonville Prison, if I had left myself time and breath to tell it. 'Oh, my!' (as old Helen used to say) 'how expensive!' prisoners costing £50 a year each. You may fancy their accommodations are somewhat remarkable. In each cell I saw a pretty little corner cupboard, on one shelf of which was the dressing apparatus – a comb and brush, and small tooth comb! – laid on a neatly folded-up towel; a shaving jug with metal top on one side, an artistic soap-box on the other! In one cell I remarked a blue tassel, with a bit of steel chain attached to it, hung from a brass nail. 'What is the use of that tassel?' I asked the inspector. 'That tassel, ma'm? why that tassel is – a fancy of the prisoner's own; we allow them to have their little fancies!' They all wear masks when in each other's presence, that, should they afterwards meet in society, their feelings may be spared. They have such charming bathrooms! Each man has a good-sized court all to himself to run about in for an hour at a time; and while we were there they all 'went to school', with books and slates under their arms, masked! If any man wishes to have the comforts of life and be taught, and 'have his fancies' let him rush out and commit a felony!

So seriously did the authorities take the separate system that in 1846 a crank was invented at Pentonville for individual use in cellular prisons; the confined prisoners did their crank labour by turning the handle of an iron drum which caused a series of cups to scoop up sand.

Winston Churchill's Visit

After Winston Churchill, then Home Secretary in the Liberal Government, visited Pentonville in 1910 and saw boy prisoners committed for petty theft and assault, he took steps to see that boy offenders, apart from exceptional cases, were excluded from prison altogether. As Lucy Masterman recalled, 'Winston is very much interested in the subject of boy prisoners at present, and their case, in spite of the Borstal system and the Children's Bill, is undeniably scandalous. A great number of boys were in prison merely for sleeping out, that is, having no homes; and more for what is put down as "obscene language" which in most cases was nothing more than putting out their tongues at the police.'

Executions

Several death sentences were carried out at Pentonville before the abolition of capital punishment in 1965; the most well known being the hanging of Sir Roger Casement in 1916 for treason after landing in Ireland from a German submarine shortly before the Easter Rising. Casement remained a hero for the Irish, and in 1965 his remains were repatriated to Ireland where a state funeral took place.

MICHAEL FARADAY

To the rear of Pentonville Prison, at the corner of Bride Street and Barnsbury Grove was a Sandemanian chapel, taken over by the North telephone exchange in 1906. From 1862 until his death in 1867 Michael Faraday, a pioneer in electricity, was an elder at this chapel. During these years Sir Alfred Yarrow, the marine engineer and shipbuilder, lived in Barnsbury as a boy. He so admired Faraday that he used to attend the services to hear him preach; he and a friend would walk in the opposite direction to that taken by Faraday and his wife on their way to chapel so that they could raise their hats as they passed Faraday; not content with doing this once, they would double round a side street to meet Faraday again. This boyish enthusiasm so amused Faraday, then in his seventies, that he would smile back or say a few kind words to them! There is a memorial tablet in the wall near the platform Faraday usually occupied when preaching, and on the floor a brass plate indicates where his pew was.

In Hollingsworth Street nearby, Mary Tealby took pity on stray dogs and started her Home for Lost and Starving Dogs in 1860, which moved to Battersea in 1871.

ST MARY MAGDALENE

Set in four or five acres, between Liverpool Road and Holloway Road, with trees interspersed with vaults, is the church of St Mary Magdalene. This was at first a chapel of ease to St Mary's parish church. The curious hump-backed building, which Elizabeth and Wayland Young say looks like a cow getting up, caused some heated debate when it was built in 1814 – not so much for its appearance but for its cost of £33,000, which exceeded the amount authorized by Parliament. The squat tower with its stone balustrade, and lacking a spire, cost the parishioners six times as much as 'the beautiful, classical and unrivalled spire of Islington church'. Nelson in 1823 remarked that 'the great elevation of the roof, from the walls to the apex, gives to the structure a truly misshapen and hump-backed appearance'. But the money seems to have been well spent on the interior of this church by William Wickings, where Tuscan columns support the galleries and the pulpit is of magnificent mahogany.

HOLLOWAY PRISON

Approached from Hillmarton Road, the front of Holloway Prison in Parkhurst Road is like a solid medieval castle only wanting a moat and drawbridge. The central tower is in fact a copy of the Caesar's Tower, Warwick Castle – an imposing example of the scene-shifting with which the Victorians adorned their institutions. James Bunning, architect of the Caledonian market, designed the prison in 1851 with radiating wings on the model of Pentonville. It was built by the Corporation of London on land intended for the burial of cholera victims of the 1830s. By 1857 it was admired by prison administrators for keeping the most complete form of separation of all the prisons inspected. Whenever prisoners moved in single file in the prison or exercise yards, they had to keep at least three yards apart, with their hands behind their backs, looking straight ahead; if they should nevertheless be able to see the chief warder, they had to give him a military salute as they passed! In 1878 the Government took over the prison but the City held on to the surplus land, by then greatly increased in value, though the Home Secretary insisted on a belt of twenty feet round the outside of the perimeter walls! Holloway

'Warwick Castle,' the front of Holloway Prison

became a prison for women only in 1903; the first woman governor, Dame Charity Taylor, was appointed in 1945. More than a hundred years after the foundation stone was laid with the inscription 'May God preserve the City of London, and make this place a terror to evil doers', the prison is to be rebuilt as a hospital prison for offenders not sent to open prisons.

Through the gates of Holloway Prison, with the emblems of the City of London, many 'evil doers' have passed to serve their sentences. William Thomas Stead, editor of the *Pall Mall Gazette*, was imprisoned here in 1885 for paying a procuress to supply him with a thirteen-year-old girl, in order to expose the trafficking of young girls described in 'the Maiden Tribute of Modern Babylon'. Though the jury added the rider that he had acted from 'the purest of motives' he was found guilty of abduction. Oscar Wilde, while awaiting trial in the 1890s, was visited here by Lord Alfred Douglas who later recalled in his *Autobiography* that this was 'the only bright spot in the day' for Wilde who looked at him with 'tears running down his cheeks'. Dr Jameson, leader of an abortive raid on Johannesburg in 1895, was committed to Holloway for six months before returning to the Cape Colony where he became Prime Minister in 1904. During the Second World War Holloway served as an internment camp and Sir Oswald Mosley was detained here under Regulation 18B. Christine Keeler served her sentence at Holloway in 1963.

DR CRIPPEN'S MURDER

On the site of Margaret Bondfield House in Hilldrop Crescent

Dr Crippen and Ethel le Neve in the dock in 1910

stood the semi-detached villa into which moved Dr Hawley
Harvey Crippen and his second wife, Cora Turner, in 1905. He
was an 'insignificant-looking little man, small and short and
slight in stature, with a sandy moustache, prominent eyes, gold-
rimmed spectacles, and large domed forehead'. He had come
from America to manage a business advertising patent medicines.
Cora Crippen, a plump, lively brunette, had little success in
establishing herself as a music-hall star under the name 'Belle
Elmore' despite the dazzling dresses, singing lessons and impul-
sive hospitality on which she splashed her money, and the couple
had an impossible domestic life. Crippen felt more for his secretary, Ethel le Neve, who was methodical and lady-like and became
his mistress. After a New Year's Eve party at their house, Crippen
poisoned his wife and interred some of the remains in the cellar.
Later he and Ethel le Neve sailed for Antwerp on their way to
Canada; after reading reports of the discovery of the body, the
captain radioed Scotland Yard (the first use of radio for police
purposes) and the couple were arrested by a detective who boarded
the ship. Crippen was executed at Pentonville in 1910, devoted to
Ethel le Neve to the last, and asked that her portrait should be
buried with him.

THOMAS JAMES WISE

For all but six years between 1860 and 1890 Thomas James Wise,
the literary forger, lived at Axminster (then Devonshire) Road.
Because of his delicate health he was brought up largely at home;
later, as a clerk, he foraged for books on the Farringdon Street
barrows and began collecting first editions. At the age of twenty-
five when Wise was earning less than £4 a week he was able to
pay £45, then a record price, for a copy of *Adonais* published in
1821, and from the library of books he started in Axminster
Road, he eventually established a valuable collection which he
called the Ashley Library. Some three years before he died in 1937
some fifty 'first editions' catalogued by him were shown to be
frauds, and after his death he was exposed as a forger.

ARCHWAY

The northern entrance to Islington is under the iron bridge

Sir Alexander Binnie, which in 1897 replaced the Archway designed by John Nash. This was built to carry Hornsey Road over the new road by-passing Highgate Village, after the brick-arched tunnel collapsed in 1812. The milestone at the foot of Highgate Hill marks the traditional spot where Dick Whittington heard Bow Bells telling him to turn again. Perched on top of the stone is a bronze cat by Jonathan Kenworthy and Tony South-well – an illustration of a legend becoming fact! The sculpture of Whittington's legendary cat was sponsored in 1964 by Donald Bisset, the children's author, after he discovered the absence of the cat.

WHITTINGTON HOSPITAL

There have been several milestones – the present one was erected in 1869 by Richard Perkins, landlord of the former Whittington Stone Tavern. Originally this stone marked the site of a leper cross associated with the first hospital here for lepers. This was the Highgate Spytell built in 1473 on land given by Edward IV to William Pole, a Yeoman of the Crown, who was a leper.

By Elizabethan times the hospital had become a spital or poor house and was said to be built with 'timber and Flemish wall, and covered with tile, and newly white-washed, consisting of one small kitchen, and another small room adjoining; also on the south end of the said house two more small rooms below stairs, and two very small chambers over them; and over the aforesaid hall and kitchen three more small chambers. Also one orchard and garden very well planted, which said house standeth on a pleasant hill in good air'.

Two wings of the Whittington Hospital are in Islington; the Gothic towering block of the Archway wing dating from the 1870s and St Mary's, formerly a smallpox hospital.

CHURCH OF ST JOHN THE EVANGELIST

The church of St John the Evangelist in Pemberton Gardens is one of the four Charles Barry designed in Islington; apparently he destroyed every drawing relating to these first Gothic churches and, it is said, would have still more gladly destroyed the buildings. St John the Evangelist is much the same as when it was built in

1826. The central box-pews and central pulpit have gone; and a later heavily carved altar and reredos have been added. The box-pews and galleries facing the brightly coloured east window by W. Bacon have a certain soberness about them; and there are two interesting monuments by Sievier to Martha and Anne, both daughters of Nicholas Sykes.

Bibliography

Arundell, D., *The Story of Sadler's Wells, 1683–1964*, Hamish Hamilton, 1965.

Binns, P. L., *The Story of the Royal Tournament*, Gale & Polden, 1952.

Bull, Leonard, *History of the Smithfield Club from 1798–1925* [the Club], 1926.

Clarke, Basil F. L., *Parish Churches of London*, Batsford, 1966.

Clunn, Harold P., *The Face of London*, Spring Books, 1961.

Committee on Housing in Greater London. *Report*. H.M.S.O., 1965 (*Cmnd. 2605. Chairman: Sir Milner Holland*).

Compton, William Bingham, *6th Marquis of Northampton, History of the Comptons of Wynyates*, Bodley Head, 1930.

Coull, Thomas, *The History and Traditions of Islington*, T. Miles, 1861.

Cromwell, Thomas, *History of the Parish of Clerkenwell*, Longmans and others, 1828.

Cromwell, Thomas, *Walks through Islington*, Sherwood, 1836.

Dare, R. A., *A History of Owen's School*, Carwal, 1963.

Dawson, William, *A Mid-London Parish*, T. G. Johnson, 1885.

Disher, Maurice W., *Pleasures of London*, Hale, 1950.

Emmons, Robert, *The Life and Opinions of Walter Richard Sickert*, Faber, 1941.

Finsbury Borough Council, Official Guide, various editions.

Gough, J. W., *Sir Hugh Myddelton: Entrepreneur and Engineer*, O.U.P., 1964.

Grant, Douglas, *The Cock Lane Ghost*, Macmillan, 1965.

Grossmith, George, and Weedon, *The Diary of a Nobody*, Penguin Books, 1965.

Hobhouse, Hermione, *Thomas Cubitt, Master Builder*, Macmillan, 1971.

Holmes, M. R., *Moorfields in 1559: an engraved copper plate from the earliest known map of London . . .* H.M.S.O., 1963.

Hornsby, Tom, *Of People, Buildings and a Faith: St Mary's Parish Church, Islington*, Gloucester, British Publishing Co., 1970.

Howard, D. L., *The English Prisons*, Methuen, 1960.

Islington Borough Council, Official Guide, various editions.

Jewsbury, Eric C. O., *The Royal Northern Hospital, 1856–1956*, H. K. Lewis, 1956.

Jones, Gareth Stedman, *Outcast London: Study in the relationship between classes in Victorian society*, O.U.P., 1971.

Kent, William (ed.), *An Encyclopaedia of London*, Dent, 1937.

Lewis, Samuel, *History and Topography of the Parish of St Mary's, Islington*, Jackson, 1842.

Lucas, E. V., *The Life of Charles Lamb*, Methuen, 1921.

Macqueen-Pope, Walter, *The Melodies Linger on: the story of music hall*, Allen, 1950.

Mingard, W. Vere, *The Story of Islington and Finsbury*, Laurie, 1915.

Mitton, G. E., *Clerkenwell and St Luke's*, Black, 1906.

Morris, Terence, and Pauline, *Pentonville*, Routledge, 1963.

Nelson, John, *History, Topography and Antiquities of the Parish of St Mary's, Islington*, Nicholson, 1823.

Oakeley, Richard, *Canonbury Tower: a brief history*, Tavistock Repertory company, 1966 reprint.

Olivier, Edith, *The Eccentric Life of Alexander Cruden*, Faber, 1934.

Oswald, Arthur, *The London Charterhouse Restored*, Country Life, 1959.

Pascoe, C. E., *London of To-day: Illustrated handbook for the season*, Bemrose, 1890.

Pepys, Samuel, *Diary*, Dent, 1906 ed.

Pevsner, Nikolaus (ed.), *London (Except the Cities of London and Westminster)*, Penguin Books, 1952.

Pinks, William J., *History of Clerkenwell*, J. T. Pickburn, 1865.

Pulling, Christopher, *They Were Singing*, Harrap, 1952.

Renwick, E. D., and Williams, I. M., *A Short History of the Order of St John* [the Order], 1962.

Rothstein, Andrew, *A House on Clerkenwell Green*, Lawrence & Wishart, 1966.

Selway, Neville C., *The Regency Road: the coaching prints of James Pollard*, Faber, 1957.

Spencer, Herbert, *London's Canal: the history of Regent's Canal*, Putnam, 1961.

Spielmann, M. H., and Layard, G. S., *Kate Greenaway*, Black, 1905.

Stow, John, *Survey of London* (reprinted from the text of 1603), O.U.P., 1908.

Summerson, Sir John, *Georgian London*, Pelican Books, 1969.

Tomlins, Thomas E., *Yseldon: a Perambulation of Islington*, Hodson, 1861.

Walker, G. Goold, *The Honourable Artillery Company, 1537–1947*, Gale & Polden, 1954.

Wroth, W., and A. E., *The London Pleasure Gardens of the Eighteenth Century*, Macmillan, 1896.

Yeandle, W. H., *A Corner of Finsbury: the History of . . . St. Clement, City Road*, W. Knott, 1934.

Young, Elizabeth, and Wayland, *Old London Churches*, Faber, 1956.

Young, Filson (ed.), *Trial of Hawley Harvey Crippen*, Hodge, 1950.

Index